◆ ◆ ◆

ASSORTED NUTS

◆　◆　◆

ASSORTED NUTS

My life and the "characters" whom God has allowed me to encounter

God Bless You!

[signature]

JAN EASTLAND

© 2012 Jan Eastland
All rights reserved.
ISBN-13: 9781977538345
ISBN-10: 1977538347
Library of Congress Control Number: 2017915285
CreateSpace Independent Publishing Platform
North Charleston, South Carolina

CONTENTS

◈ ◈ ◈

DEDICATION AND ACKNOWLEDGMENTS

Dedicated to Mama Sue, Elsye Eastland,
Bob Utley, and Margie,
Mattie Muriel and Mikal Cox

This book is dedicated to my grandmother, Mama Sue Eastland, who raised me from infancy until I was nineteen years old. In my eyes, she was a saint. She devoted her entire life to me without any signs of resentment. She was such a gentle person. Her husband died at the early age of 30, and she had to raise three boys by herself during the Depression. Her boys all grew up to be fine, well-adjusted citizens.

My daddy died when I was ten years old from a sudden heart attack. Mama Sue stayed at home with me and never left my side. She was a great comfort to my mother after my daddy died. She did the cooking, washing, and housecleaning while my mother worked. She was admired and loved by all who knew her. She loved me dearly and had more patience with me than anyone else could ever have had. If I am a success today, it is because of her and the love that she instilled in me. Since her death, many people have said, "Whoever raised you sure did a fantastic job on you!" She brought me up with a fantastic attitude, always expecting me to do my best. I am looking forward to being with her again in Heaven.

Won't that be a fantastic day! God has surely blessed my life by sending her my way.

My mother had an impact on my life, too. She took over when Mama Sue died. Mama Sue and my mother will both get a crown in Heaven for what they have done for me. They and others accepted me as I was. They were never ashamed of me, and I am truly grateful for that.

My grade school, junior high, high school classmates and teachers accepted me as I was and loved me. Mattie Muriel English was a wonderful friend, who "hung in there" with me through thick and thin, throughout all of my life. Mattie Muriel and her two sisters, Hortense and Frances, meant so much to me. Mattie Muriel died not so very long ago, and I miss her terribly. When she died, she left me some money to help me get my book published. The book will be a great tribute to her. I could not have had the book published without her help. She must be smiling down from Heaven, thrilled to have been a part of my life If she knew; and I think she does know.

The wonderful people of Haskell, Texas, gave me encouragement, love, and devotion when I needed it most.

The young people and professors at Hardin-Simmons University accepted me with open arms and encouraged me to keep on keeping on. I could never have made it without them. I want to thank my friends, teachers, and my professors. I love each and every one of them very much.

My family hung in there and supported me with love. God was a source of constant help for me. I also want to thank Bob Utley and Margie, our church secretary, for helping me put my erasable tape in my typewriter, because I couldn't do it. I could not have written this book without their help.

John and Wanda Rogers have been helpful with the book and many other ways. Beth Woods has given me much support and love by taking me to see my mother in the nursing home. I will always love her for that. Hazel Howe and Charlotte Bridges have both been helpful with the book, and in many other ways, too. Mikal Cox has given me money to help with the book. Mike Eastland bought me a new hard drive for my computer, so I could get my book published. Mike Foster has done some work on my computer which was very helpful."

◆ ◆ ◆

PREFACE

My name is Jan Eastland, and I am a cerebral palsy victim. Principally this story is an autobiography showing what I have been able to accomplish, because my Parents and Friends accepted me as an individual and encouraged me always to do my best. The following poem illustrates my attitude toward my accomplishments:

"If a task is once begun,
Never leave it 'til it's done.
Be the labor great or small,
Do it well or not at all."

The purpose of this book is to send a message to parents of handicapped babies and children. Do not feel guilty or blame yourself, if your child is handicapped in any way. It takes a special person or persons to raise a handicapped child and God chooses special parents for his special little ones. Do not pity your child or make him feel inferior, because he is different. Find out what he/she can do and encourage him/her to do his/her best.

Many children today are born daily with some type of handicap, and there are many kinds of handicaps. In fact, if you look around at "normal" people (including yourself), you will note that almost everyone has some type of minor handicap.

The world would be a sad place, indeed, if some "handicapped" people had not lived. For example:

1. Thomas Edison was not allowed to go to public school, because his teachers thought his lack of intelligence did not merit their time and effort. His mother believed in him, encouraged him, and taught him at home. Because he was a genius, we owe the electric lights, movies, phonograph and other inventions to him. In fact, when he was grown he was called "The "Wizard of Menlo Park."
2. Albert Einstein was considered to be mentally retarded until he was almost grown. Instead, his genius was considered to be a handicap, because it was not "normal." Yet now he is considered the smartest man of the entire twentieth century. Without him, there would have been no atomic bomb or other atomic developments.
3. Winston Churchill, the great British Statesman, did not learn to talk until he was about seven years old.
4. Fox Beyer's handicap was cerebral palsy, and he became a champion baseball pitcher.
5. There are countless others -- too numerous to name.

So, parents do not "let" your child be handicapped. Just treat your child as any ordinary individual, and you will be blessed.

Chapter 1

❖ ❖ ❖

MY EARLY YEARS
AND THE EFFECT THE ASSORTMENT OF FAMILY
"NUTS" HAD ON MY CHILDHOOD

This book is entitled *Assorted Nuts* because that's what I lovingly call a collection of friends accumulated throughout my life. I attract them like honey attracts bees. Thanks to a great sense of humor, I've been able to "handle what I handle," and thusly have become the "nuttiest nut" of them all! Okay, I'll cut myself some slack calling myself a "mixed nut." I guess I am all kinds of nuts rolled into one. On a serious note, though, I emphasize that the purpose of this book is to urge parents of handicapped children to treat them as normally as possible, and NOT to feel guilty.

I am a very lucky person, with so many people interested in and supportive of me. I care about people; they care about me. One such person is Marshall J. Pierson, Jr., of Corpus Christi, Texas. He attended Haskell High School with my mother in 1929. He was kind to write the following about me, though it was never published:

"This is a story, a true story, of a most remarkable person. A story that I wish to share with those who do not know it. There are two people, who dared to dream the impossible dream, and their

determination and faith in a wonderful God changed the impossible to possible, and then, into fact. Those two people are Jan and her mother, Elsye."

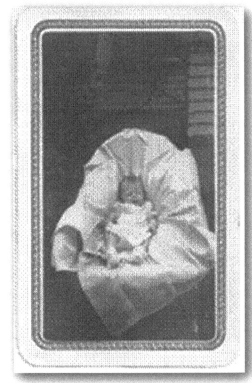

Baby Jan, Haskell Texas, 1943

I was born in a Catholic hospital in Garden City, Kansas, on June 23, 1943, the daughter of Elsye Bradley Eastland and Doyle Lee Eastland. They both were from a long line of strong willed people. I am a victim of cerebral palsy due to a birth injury. Cerebral palsy means brain damage. My mother had a terrible time during labor. The nurses told her later that the attending doctor was drunk. They had to sober him up for the delivery. We could have sued him, but couldn't prove his negligence. I wish they hadn't told my mother. (My birth should have been by Cesarean section, but such was seldom done in those days.)

I have since wondered what happened to that doctor, and if he had any idea of the damage he caused my mother, family and me. My mother had to stay in the hospital 21 days. My daddy came to see us at night, always telling her that the nurses were playing with me out in the hall. The nurses pampered me with special treatment and colorful dresses, spoiling me greatly before we were released from the hospital.

Frank and Mary Anna McMahan were good friends; Daddy and Frank were in the Air Force together. Mary Anna often came to see us and play with me, and I'd laugh and laugh. Everyone wants to know why I'm such a "nut." I tell them, "If you could see who I started out with, you'd know why." Mary Anna and Frank liked to "cut up" and act silly. I loved them; they were special people who, upon moving to Lubbock, kept in touch with us through the years. They'd visit us -- and vice versa -- and their three children -- Leigh Ann, Ronald and Gary -- worshiped the ground I walked on. I have never been so loved, and was privileged to spend two weeks with them during summers. They are all grown and married and have children of their own now. Leigh Ann still lives in Lubbock. I can still see her and her family, but the boys live far away. I treasure the memories we shared together. The entire family provided important influences on my life, even to this day. They loved and accepted me as I was—and as I am.

Mama Sue, Jan and Elyse, 1944

Mother and I lived in Colorado City, Texas, for a while before moving to Haskell. That's where we landed after Daddy and Frank were sent off to Germany to serve in World War II. Daddy was discharged in December, 1945.

The motor part of my brain was injured. At first, I walked on my tiptoes, holding on to someone's hand, but I also wanted to be able to climb stairs. My parents took me to Dallas, Texas, to see Dr. Brandon Carroll, head surgeon at Scottish Rite Hospital. He recommended surgery on my legs to lengthen the ligaments. At first, I wore braces on my legs and feet at night while sleeping. One night, I fell off the bed, frightening my mother, even though I didn't even wake up. Later, when Dr. Carroll performed surgery on me, I was quite scared. The nurses promised me a chicken if I would be good. I was, but never saw the chicken! Promises should be kept! We stayed with my Great-Aunt Ann and Great-Uncle Arnold, while in Dallas. We've visited them regularly over the years, and I love them both dearly.

Jan, with casts on her feet, following surgery.

After the casts came off, I asked Dr. Carroll to come outside and watch me climb stairs. He did so, commenting that my surgery was "more successful than any he had ever seen." I walked like everyone else, and I learned to ride a bicycle. A friend heard me tell my granddad I was going to learn to ride a bicycle. It made such an impression on her she told me later she would never again doubt it when I said I was going to do something.

Daddy went into the insurance business for a while, until his partner ran off with all of his money. Then he was elected County Treasurer, public service that ended with declaration of war. Mother worked as a telephone operator during and following the war. She told me she remembered the day Pearl Harbor was bombed, because the telephone lines were really busy. Later, she worked for the Department of Agriculture for 25 years. Daddy became hospital administrator until he died. It was extremely stressful work.

There was no West Texas Rehabilitation Center in Abilene at the time, and the nearest facility was in Lubbock. My parents couldn't make the trip regularly, but I took private lessons to improve my speech and tap dancing to help my coordination. The latter included playing a clown in a play, in a hot costume yet!

When I had my tonsils removed, I again greatly feared the surgery. A bear of a surgeon, one Dr. Kimbrough, loved me dearly and I loved him. He was a "hugger." I knew he'd never hurt me, but he always seemed so huge to me. They don't make doctors like him anymore!

Everyone in my family had a sense of humor; this helped them to accept me, despite my infirmities. Such acceptance means more than I can express. If the child's family loves and accepts the child, the child will be a success, no matter what he or she has to overcome. I was very lucky in this regard. There were five children in mother's family. My Grandad and Grandmother Bradley loved me and accepted me, and I loved them.

When I was ten, daddy died of a heart attack. I awoke one morning to people crying before learning of his death during the night at age 40. They said I was "too young to understand," but I knew I'd never see my daddy again in this life. I look forward to seeing him again in heaven. I didn't really understand his death until years later, but it made my mother's life much tougher. My Granddad Bradley was a character, and it took only a short time for him to take my daddy's place in my heart. Of course, I have never forgotten my daddy, and know he would have been pleased to know that I had Granddad Bradley giving me such loving care.

Jan with her mother, Elyse Bradley Eastland, and her father,
Doyle Lee Eastland

Granddad was a "pecan nut." He said some of the funniest things I wish had been written down. I loved sitting on his lap and laughing at his funny stories. Once I asked Mother if she thought all of his stories were true. "I don't know for sure, but I do know he's been telling the same stories for years," Mother said. I remember his asking once if I knew the rabbit used to have a long tail and the dog could talk? He said the dog was chasing the rabbit and went under some barbed wire fence, and after that. the rabbit had a short tail and the dog could only bark." I worshipped my Granddad Bradley. He really defied description..

Mother's sister, Vera, married Luther Cummings. Vera is a *butternut*. Granddad and Grandmother Bradley raised five children during the depression. They all turned out very well. Vera and Luther had a daughter, Kay, and a son, Kent (grandmother's maiden name). Kay and I spent summers together that I will always treasure. She lives in Azle, Texas, and has one married son, Matt. Kent married Norma, a precious person; they have a daughter, Julie, and a son, Carson. We lost Kent to a heart attack. Carson married Marla and they have two daughters. Julie Kay is also married and has a son.

When I think of Vera and all the fun we had, I remember when Vanna Lee sent Vera a chain letter. Vera said that she wished Vanna Lee had not sent her a chain letter, because it was against the law. Well, after Vera and Luther went home, the wheels in my mind started turning. I thought to myself, "Wouldn't it be funny to send Vera a letter from a judge telling her that she was to appear in court on charges of mail fraud?" I asked mother if she thought Vera would fall for it, and Mother said she didn't think she would. I wrote her a most business like letter, except I didn't put a letterhead on it. A few days later we got a phone call from Vera saying she was going to court on charges of mail fraud and for me not to send out anymore letters. Mother turned to me and said, "Oh! Vera thinks that letter is for real!" I then confessed, telling her I'd sent the letter and made up the judge's name. You could hear a sigh of relief on the other end of the phone!

Mother's other sister, Dodie, never got married. She lived and worked on the farm with granddad and grandmother. One time a bull got after her, and she cleared the fence, thanks to her long legs! She took care of the grandparents Bradley until they died, both in their 80s. Dodie, too, is now deceased.

Harry, another of mother's brothers, was mentally ill for 60 years. He brought a lot joy into my life. His wife, Artie, was a jewel. Harry left me with a great understanding and compassion for mentally ill people, and how mental disabilities affect entire families.

Cecil was another of mother's brothers, and he was a mess! Cecil and Vanna Lee were "litchi nuts" because no matter how much you tried, you couldn't get rid of them! Vanna Lee was a widow when Cecil married her. She had two children in a former marriage, Jimmy and Van L. Vanna Lee brightened my life a lot. She told stories that got bigger and bigger. We really had fun when they came to town. Cecil delighted in teasing people. He used to play paper dolls with his sisters until he tired of it. Then, he'd cut off the dolls' heads! He "baptized" Dodie's doll in the horses' water trough, ruining it. Cecil picked on me every minute we were together, and I loved it. I became an expert telling Cecil "To Shut Up." Every time I told him, he'd laugh riotously.

Cecil's friend in Pampa, a man named Travis, dressed like a pauper and cut his own hair. However, people thought he had plenty of money stuffed in his mattress. I saw him at times, when we visited, puzzled that he didn't even have running water in his little house. He'd borrow water from his neighbors. One day, the pastor at First Baptist Church, were Travis worked as a janitor, caught him bathing in the baptistery. No doubt the parson was shocked.

It was known that Travis loved the bottle. One day the sheriff caught him driving drunk. He pulled him over and chewed him out, but it didn't do any good. Cecil loved to tease me about Travis, claiming Travis was my boyfriend. Sometimes Travis cut grass for extra money. One day, Cecil reached his hand into my pocket, then he opened his hand, saying, "See there! There are grass snips in your pocket." Of course, there was nothing in his hand. "Can you explain that?" Cecil asked. "See there! You have been messing around with Travis again." I told him to shut up. Another time, a very rich man gave me a brand new typewriter, and after he left, Cecil said, "Are you going to put Travis's name on your new typewriter?"

I wish I could remember more that Cecil said about Travis and me! Travis has died, and I always wondered what he did with all of his money…

That reminds me of a story about Mother and the Haskell County sheriff. I was having trouble sleeping, which is nothing unusual. I have always had problems sleeping. Some cerebral palsied people sleep, and some do not. I hate being in the latter group. I am looking forward to heaven, so I can rest. Anyway, the doctor suggested my mother give me some wine before I went to sleep. She went to the sheriff, asking if she could buy some wine. "Elsye, I can't do that, they'd get me for bootleg-ging!" The wine didn't help anyway. It just made me more hyper.

I didn't know Grandmother Bradley's family very well; they lived far away. I know I would have loved them, too. I've heard stories about them. I knew and loved Jack and Helen Cobb. Jack is a "nut." Jack and Helen were on Grandmother Bradley's side of the family. I loved Aunt Mary, Aunt Ernie, Aunt Johnny, Aunt Louie, Uncle Jim, Uncle Ira and Aunt Charity. They were among Granddad Bradley's clan.

Aunt Charity lived to be 101 years old. She took Grandmother's place in my heart after my grandmother died. She resided in the Haskell rest home for 40 years. She was an inspiration to me and to a lot of other people. I loved to listen to her stories about living in the rest home.

I loved Aunt Mary and Uncle Jim, too. Uncle Jim sent me birthday cards I have kept for years. He was a true character. Aunt Mary, now deceased, used to give bridge parties in her home, and she loved to play practi-cal jokes on people. One time, she put a male dummy in her bathroom, where, of course, a female guest was frightened! Another time, she put the dummy's leg under the bed, and another guest thought there was a dead body underneath! Yet another time, she put a rubber snake in her neighbor's yard, then hid in the bushes while he "chopped it up" with a hoe. A favorite was her placement of a "For Sale" in her neighbors' yard when they were on vacation….

Aunt Mary's granddaughter, Mary Kay, played on the TV show, *Mary Hartman! Mary Hartman!* I told some neighborhood kids that Mary Kay

Place was my cousin. One day, walking my dog, some kids followed me around, asking about Mary Kay Place. I confirmed regularly, "Yes, she's really my cousin." I told them her grandmother lived in Rule, TX. They wanted to know if she had a boyfriend, and I answered that I didn't know. (A few questions aren't "fit" for a family book!) We are very proud of cousin Mary, who recently was in a movie called "Sweet Home, Alabama." She also has been in numerous other shows, and stays in touch by phone.

My Granddad Eastland died when daddy was three years old; therefore, I didn't know him. I have been told he was a fine man with a keen a sense of humor. My daddy must have inherited some of that humor. Mama Sue raised three boys, Rae, Holt, and Doyle, during the Depression. Doyle was my daddy. Holt married Effie, and they had two sons named Tommy and Barry. Barry was killed in a car wreck at the age of 15. We all loved Barry very much, and we miss him. Tom married Sue, and they had three children, Mark, Steve, and Tommy Sue, all now grown and married. Tommy Sue is a policewoman now. I never knew them very well. I wish I had....

Holt is an "almond nut" because he could say some of the funniest things. I used to follow him around, probably running him *nuts*! One day, I was standing under the air conditioner he was working on. "Some old bird has his arm in the way," he said, talking to himself. He was working on my air conditioner, and I was standing right under his nose. Holt said, "Some old bird has his arm in the way." Though he was talking to himself, he said it because he knew I'd laugh, and I did! Steve, Mark, and Tommy Sue have children of their own now. After Effie died, Holt married a woman named Estelle, and they live in Victoria, Texas. Holt and Estelle are both now deceased.

Rae married Hazel; the latter is a "hazel nut." Rae is now dead. One time Hazel was driving from Dallas to Stamford, and she was driving really fast. A policeman gave chase, but she wouldn't slow down. She she finally stopped and he asked why she was driving so fast? She said it was because she was so scared to be out on the road by herself." He didn't issue a ticket. Another time, while driving from Stamford to Abilene, she was speeding again—and chased again. Noticing a funeral procession on the highway near Hawley, she joined it. At the cemetery, she joined the family under the tent to avoid a ticket. The policeman, watching her from the highway, laughed so hard he decided not to give her a citation. Hazel said she didn't know the deceased or anyone at the cemetery.

Hazel and Rae's children were Bill, Mike and Rebecca Sue. Bill married Billie Nell; they had twin boys, Ross and Rae. Bill and Billie Nell now live in San Angelo. Ross and Rae both attended college and are now working. Rae married Lisa, and Ross married Shay, and they had a boy, William Conrad, and a girl, Callie. Rae and Lisa have two daughters, Sarah and Kate. Rae works for an investment company and Ross works for a computer company.

Mike married Vicki. He was my "kissing cousin" until I embarrassed him in front of my best girlfriend. He turned red in the face. I just did it for meanness. He'd make all kinds of faces at me when we were children, and, of course, I would laugh. Mike said later that I got him into trouble; but if he had not been making faces at me, I wouldn't have been laughing at him. He was the City Manager of Carrollton, Texas, at one time, but now is the Executive Director of the North Central Texas Council of Governments. We are very proud of him. Vicki taught school for years. She still works for the school on special projects, such as school trips. Mike and Vicki's children are Staci and Julie. Staci works in a doctor's office in Chicago. Staci is now married to Pete. They have three children -- Nicole, Olivia, and Tommy. Staci is going back to school. Julie is a Lt. Colonel in the Marines. Julie is married to Eric; he is a graduate of the FBI school.

Rebecca Sue married Sam and they have two children -- J.J. and Eric. When he was three years old, Eric asked me, "Why do you talk the way you do?" I said, "What do you mean?" And Eric retorted, "You heard me!" (He was very smart for his age) I told him to ask his mother, because she could explain it better than I could. I thought what he asked me was very funny, and when he gets older, I'm going to tell him what he asked me. Sam and Rebecca lived in Stanford, Texas, and Rebecca Sue teaches

Special Education. Sam farmed until the farming business played out. Then he owned a funeral home. Rebecca Sue and J.J. live in San Angelo now, and Eric lives with his father. Then Rebecca Sue married Tommy, and since then they have moved to the Dallas-Fort Worth area. Tommy is in construction work. J.J. is now married to Justin, and they have a baby boy. They also live in the Dallas-Fort Worth area.

My Grandmother Eastland was a fantastic lady. Everyone who knew her loved her. If anyone said a cross word about her, I don't recall it. In this day and time, mothers have a hard time raising children by themselves, but they do not have the qualities Mama Sue had. If she could do it back then: they could do it today. This book is dedicated to Mama Sue Eastland, and the love she instilled in me. She helped raise me after daddy died, and I was worse than the three boys; I was into everything! She devoted her entire life to me. She was a lot of help to my mother. She supported her with love and encouragement.

Mother and Mama Sue got along really well, perhaps unusual for two women in the same house. They always reminded me of Ruth and Naomi in the Bible. I never heard a cross word between them, except one time when mother was sick. I know that sounds unlikely, but it is the truth.

I slept with Mama Sue, and I don't know how she managed it. I didn't sleep well, tossing and turning all night. Consequently, she didn't get any sleep either. That's why her patience never ceased to amaze me. If she ever lost patience with me, she didn't show it. She loved me, whatever it took. I was a hyperactive child, flying "off the handle" every once in a while. Mama Sue called me "Old Blue Hen's Pullet." Mama Sue said I reminded her of a chicken, who was about to flog someone. Her love for me was amazing! She died when I was a freshman at HSU. If she could see me now, she'd know her patience paid off!

She also kept my cousin, Bill Eastland, when he was little, because his mother had tuberculosis. Bill was hyper, too. One day Hazel asked him, "Well, Bill, what kind of day did you have?" Bill said, "Not a very good day." Hazel asked, "Why?" He replied that Mama Sue had spanked him. Bill said, "It was sure a surprise! I didn't think she would do it." (Bill couldn't say surprise). Bill had done everything that day -- he had put the cat in the mailbox, crawled under the house, and probably even more! He just pushed Mama Sue too far. That's why Bill said, "It sure was a surprise!" Mama Sue hardly ever lost her temper.

My mother was a better-than-average mother, but she was human. I didn't realize how lucky I was until years later when I worked with the children at the Rehab Center and saw what kind of families some of them had. They didn't deal with their guilt very well. Some of the parents neglected their children. Everyone with a handicapped child has guilt—the worse the handicap, the deeper the guilt.

Mother felt especially guilty about my being handicapped, since the doctor who brought me into this world was drunk. He ruined her health as well. We stayed in the hospital in Garden City, Kansas, for 21 days. She concealed her guilt to everyone except Mama Sue and me, but this guilt led her into a life of frustration and depression. She also had low self-esteem; this only made things worse. I couldn't handle her being frustrated and depressed all the time, but she was happy some of the time. This is what makes it so hard on us as children; we don't want our parents to feel bad.

I have had two mothers. Both did a lot for me, then they "undid" a great deal by what they said. Neither realized what was happening to me; it was not good. I know mothers are human, but I have never could understand why they couldn't see what they were doing to me. I saw what they did.

My mother felt if she had gone to another doctor, maybe I wouldn't have been a cerebral palsied person, and she wouldn't have such bad health. I would have felt much better, though, if she had not been so frustrated and depressed. Her being happier, in turn, would have made me happy, too. I was as happy as I could be under the circumstances, but it could have been so much better for both of us. Oh, I can see now why she was that way. I couldn't see it as a child, but when I grew up, I began to understand it. When my daddy died at such an early age, it made things harder on both of us. Thank goodness, however, we still had Mama Sue.

If my daddy, Doyle, had lived, everything would have been different. Mother was mad at daddy, because he left her with such a heavy load. I don't blame her; I would have been mad at him, too. His sudden death was senseless. My Aunt Vera said he "gave too much blood at the hospital." He was Hospital Administrator at that time. I have said many times that daddy had better change his name in heaven, because when mother dies, she is going to kill him for leaving me to raise by herself. Then I am going to kill him, when I die, for going off and leaving me with mother. Daddy will have to die three times. I can just picture that in my mind. Of course, this will never happen, but I

Jan's paternal Grandmother Eastland (affectionately known as "Mama Sue") was instrumental in raising Jan from infancy to age 19.

think about it. Part of the family ignored the situation, which did not help matters much. This is typical reaction. Her family never once told mother they loved her or to "hang in there, because we'll help you." They took it for granted that she knew that, but it would have been nice for her to hear it. That was the only way they knew how to deal with it, but she needed them to be concerned about her and show they cared. One of my aunts was a "pill." That did not help much either. Not everyone on her side of the family was like that, and we were grateful. Two of my aunts on her side of the family were silly, which is what we needed most. I don't mean they didn't care, but they did not demonstrate any emotion in words. Mother was a very brave lady, but she could have used some support along the way. People can be cruel without really meaning to be. Another undeserved problem mother had, quite simply, was a bad boss. He tried to get her fired, but the County Conservation Committee told him he'd best not try it. He was a jerk, taking credit for what his staff did. He made it so hard on mother at work. Haskell citizens, however, really supported us and encouraged us.

We went to Abilene to shop, and Mother would be as happy if she could act silly, which I loved. Then, upon return home, she'd be frustrated and depressed again. Oh, if she could only have been jolly and silly most of the time, we all would have profited! Sadly, she was often mad with no reason. However, depression ruled, even at stoplights. I don't think she realized it, used to putting up a front. That is usually what people do. I have had people tell me, just since we moved to Abilene, that they could tell she was depressed. After Daddy died, she forgot herself and con-centrated totally on my happiness. This didn't do either of us any good. Grieving people need to go through their own heartaches to make them more understanding of others. My Grandmother Eastland lived with us, and Mother could have gone out at night, but she wouldn't. If she had, it might have helped a great deal. I did not tie her down—she tied herself down. My Granddad Bradley provided much support to mother and me; it helped a great deal.

Mary was a counselor at Abilene First Baptist Church. She was very good at her job. We were in a group setting and it was very interesting and informative. I was very depressed about losing my job at the Rehab Center and worried about my future. During a talk with her about the guilt I feel parents have about their handicapped children, she suggested that I write a book about it. So I did….

Nearly every family with a handicapped child suffers from this guilt. The more handicapped the child is, the more guilt that parents have. They usually don't know how to deal with it; however, some families do better than others. The reason my mother's burden was so heavy was because my daddy died at such an early age, leaving her with total responsibility. I can clearly see how things would have been different had he lived.

Later in life, riding with one of the teachers at the Rehab Center, I learned of a family she spoke of who had a severely handicapped child. The daddy had a great sense of guilt. Sadly, the father and child died on the same day. Jackie, the teacher, said she ". . . was glad, because it was a tremendous relief to the mother." I imagine that it was a great relief. People often don't consider what is good for the child; they are thinking about themselves. I was very lucky in a lot of ways, because I never had to say that. My mother did everything she could for me, and I appreciated it, too. A person has a choice on whether to be happy or depressed. She chose to be depressed.

This book might help another parent or parents feel less guilty and make it better for another handicapped child and his/her family. You listen to me--do not make the same mistake my mother and many other mothers and fathers before her made! This is the book's main purpose.

Mother was an inspiration to many people, but she did not see that she had done more good than harm. Isn't it a shame that she was such a depressed person, when there was no need for her to be? It just made it harder on both of us. I always felt bad that mother was mad at herself, because she didn't go to college and make something out of herself. She could have done so; others in her class did. She didn't need to let depression stop her. She could have worked her way through like others in her class did. So, if all of this makes me feel badly; it makes other handicapped children feel the same way.

People are waiting for us to be happy, but we will never be completely happy, since we do not feel well, and we never will. Nobody likes to suffer. If you have cerebral palsy, you will always be sick and nervous – you simply can't help it.

Oh, we are happy some of the time. We feel worse than we appear, but we often put up fronts when going through difficult times. I don't want others to know how badly I often feel. It takes a lot of food for us, since we use up lots of energy due to our inability to remain still. Many don't understand that. I found out in later years that parents of handicapped children deal in extremes -- either neglecting their children completely, or, conversely, making them the centers of their universe. This is especially true if their spouses die, as was the case with my mother. However, it is better to err on the side of the former. Mother made me her whole life – then resented me for it. I can understand why she said I "dominated her life." It was true to a certain extent, but consider this: When we'd go out to eat, she'd insist that I decide on which restaurant, even though she didn't want to make this admission to herself, or to me.

Handicapped children can put a strain on marriage relationships, and sometimes they are damaged forever. How do you think that makes such children feel? Their sense of self-worth plummets. Many times, husbands/fathers -- as well as wives/mothers--bow to their egos, unable to accept their children's handicaps. On the other hand, I have known cases that have brought husbands and wives closer together. If my daddy had lived, I believed my condition would have eventually brought him and my mother closer together. It is saddening to believe they really loved each other, and much could have been worked through had he lived.

My mother, a nervous wreck, often avoided taking nerve medication, since many in her generation thought this to be a weakness. We'd both have been better off, however, if she'd taken her medicine.

Perhaps she couldn't help it, but she frequently spoke tacky words to me. Here again, life was made tougher for both of us. It is said that whatever is spoken to handicapped children, much care should be taken, or responses will be hurled back in kind. This is what happened to Mother and me. I made child-like errors, but it was a two-way street. She would always eventually apologize, but after she had become angry 20 times a day—day in and day out—I simply couldn't handle it. I'd think to myself, "Mother, don't you realize I can't handle it?....

Her friends in Haskell said that during high school, she was "such a happy person." That is all I really wanted her to be. Yet, through it all, I am grateful for her, simply wishing with all my heart that frustration hadn't taken over so often.

Despite her bad health, my mother never gave up. I give her that. Someone once told me I was all that kept her going. One of her co-workers informed me that when I went away to college, she became less

Jan's 12th birthday in 1955, with her Grandad and Grandmother
Bradley, Mama Sue and Aunt Dodie Bradley

interested in life than when I was at home. Yes, I know that she loved me, and I loved her. For putting up with me, she will receive a crown in heaven so heavy she won't be able to hold her head up. I brought her a lot of joy, but it breaks my heart to think how much unhappiness I brought her without intending to.

That is a reason I oppose alcoholic drinks that bring so much heartache and suffering. Even though we didn't deserve it, alcohol did much damage in every area of our lives. Drugs do even more.

Chapter 2

❖   ❖   ❖

THE ASSORTED NUTS AMONG MY CHILDHOOD FRIENDS AND PETS

Being an only child has its good points and its bad points. One of the bad points concerns loneliness. However, I played with neighborhood children. We had six teenagers on our block with whom I loved to visit. Their names included Peggy and Betty Waldrop, Pat and Ann Harrison, Pat and Kay Henry. I know I ran them nuts, even though they didn't say so. I have kept in touch with four of them, but I don't know the whereabouts of Betty and Peggy. I so wish I could see them again; we had so much fun together. Three younger friends—Donny Kay, Dianne and Charles—also enjoyed "playing store."

Charles was also hyper--like a Mexican jumping bean. We played well together, except for one memorable day when we both got into trouble. Using rocks, we scratched up a brand new car. Truly, we enjoyed the scratching! Neither of us had done that such a thing before, and we were in "double trouble."

Oleta, the car's owner, knocked on our door, fuming about the vandalism. Mother was shocked, promising that when Daddy got home from work, he'd be over to discuss the matter. The "two daddies" agreed to pay for the damages, and I was scared to the utmost! Charles and I continued to play together, but never did anything that bad again because neither of us wanted parents to be that mad at us again! Charles is now lawyer and a judge, and I wonder if he remembers this incident. Overall, though, the neighborhood children accepted me, giving me a good emotional start in life.

Paula Jo was another childhood friend of mine. I'll call her a "pistachio nut." Her grandparents lived across the street from us when I was little; she and her family lived behind the grandparents. One day, Paula saw me sitting on my front porch in my wheelchair, soon after I'd undergone leg surgery.. She came over to visit without telling her mother where she was going. When her mother missed her and learned her whereabouts, she spanked her all the way home.

Paula always said the sweetest things to me, like, "Bless your heart!" It really gave me needed lifts. Thus was started a lifelong friendship. We played mud pies, house, store, doctor and nurse together. We slid down her grandmother's cellar door until we wore holes in our panties.

Her brother Jim loved to pick on us. Her family moved to Andrews, Texas, shortly after that, but we still kept in touch. We wrote letters back and forth; I still have and treasure them. When she returned later to visit her grandparents on holidays and during summers, she always would come to see me, too.

After Daddy died, we moved across the street from her other grandparents, Granddad and Grandmother Free. Mrs. Free and Paula Jo have the same delightful sense of humor. After my own granddad and grandmother died, Mr. and Mrs. Free took their place in my heart. I loved to visit the Frees; we had great times together. Mrs. Free has passed away, but when she was still at home -- and later when she moved to the Haskell rest home -- Mother and I visited her at every opportunity.

Paula Jo is now married and has three children. She and her husband, Gene, met at Texas Tech. Gene was a very good person before he had to fight in the Vietnam War. Unfortunately, it made a wreck of him. His parents were also from Haskell. Before the children were born, they'd still visit grandparent Frees at Christmas, so I'd get to see her then. Since then, however, they've moved to New Mexico, a long way to travel with three children. Still, we are close in our hearts.

Paula Jo has no idea what she did for me at an early age. She told me I was worthy, and she gave me the confidence to overcome my insecurities. I have a picture of her that bring joy to my heart at every viewing. Another wonderful thing about our friendship is that we were lucky enough to find each other in our lifetimes. We will likewise be with each other in heaven, where there will be much joy with family and friends.

Then, there are my four-footed friends. My dogs and cats have provided great comfort to me. They have helped me through many days when I did not feel well. Sometimes, little else kept me going. My first dog was Lightning. I named her Lightning because her mother's name was Thunder. A fox terrier/rat terrier mix, she was the sweetest dog of all. She would follow wherever I went in the neighborhood, and Mother always knew I was nearby when she could see Lighting standing at our neighbors' front doors, waiting for me to come out. She was such a good-natured dog. Alas, Lightning's life was ended by a neighbor's car, perhaps because she didn't hear well. The accident greatly upset our neighbor.

Jan with her first dog, "Lightning" in 1954

My next dog was a reindeer Chihuahua named Pepi. She was a sweet dog, but she barked too much. Two of my college friends gave her to me. She was run over in New Mexico while we were visiting Bill, Billie Nell, and the boys. We spent a month in New Mexico after mother retired, and it sure was lonely without Pepie. I have learned how to stop a dog from barking. You throw a coke can at a door or a wall and tell the dog to quit barking, and after a while he or she begins to associate the noise with the barking. The dogs quit barking after a while. It really works. A friend of mine taught me that. I wish I had known that during Pepie's life.

When we got home, we got a beautiful silver poodle we named Misty, who was six weeks old. Soon he had a beautiful silver coat, but some thought he looked like a monkey when we first got him. He had coal-black eyes, but his health was hampered by poor treatment prior to our getting him. That dog loved to chase helicopters! During a walk one day, a helicopter flew overhead, quite near the ground. Misty was gone! I chased him across the school yard near my apartment complex before stopping him. I was angry with him, realizing he could have gotten run over. But, I later got tickled about his chases. He later suffered kidney failure, and we had to put him to sleep. It was hard and sad for Mother and me; she really loved the dog, too.

I got another poodle. Taffy sported a beautiful apricot color, and he was a "poodle pill!" At first, he was so hyper, into everything. When we had him neutered, he settled down a lot. Someone tried to break into my apartment awhile back. If it had not been for Taffy's barking that wakened me, I hate to think what would have happened to me and my best friend.

Taffy loved riding in the car. Charlotte and I took him with us sometimes when running errands. Every time he went with us in car, he sounded like he was talking. Charlotte once said, "I wonder what he is trying to tell us?" One day, we made a tape recording of his "voice," and, upon playing it, he barked at himself! My dogs all lived to be old, but we weren't so lucky with cats. . .

When Mother went to the rest home, I wanted another dog to keep me company. Then I got Chantilly, part dachshund, who was a pill, too!. Since her mother was little, I thought she would be little, too, but she grew to be a huge dog. When I took her walking, she would have provided free transportation if I'd had on roller skates. She barked too much, so I had to find her a new home. It nearly killed me since I loved her so much, and she loved me, too. She would put her front paws around my neck like she was hugging me. I was lucky because I found her a good home where she had three kids to love her, and a big backyard to play in. I went to see her a couple of times, and she would still put her paws around my neck. However, after they had her only six months, she was run over, and this broke our hearts. I cried because she was the first dog that I could not keep. I will never do that again because it was too hard on me. I will always love and remember Chantilly. She gave a lot of joy to the children and to me.

I made friends with the wonderful family that took Chantilly. I have become interested in their children, and I go to see them a lot. I believe Chantilly's purpose in life was to bring us together. The children's names are Rockie, Roger, and Keri. I have always been interested in children. They are our future, and are worthy of our interest and support. Ruby and J. C. are their parents; I truly love all of them.

Oh, about the cats. I had cats, too. Che was a "walnut," because he had a hard head. He was our "stand out" cat. He fought all the time and came home scarred up from fights. I should have given him the Purple Heart because he fought so much. He was a loving cat who slept in the funniest positions. Refusing to wash himself, I called him a "hippie cat.". One time we tripped on a mousetrap. It scared him to death, and he ran out of the room as fast as he could. We laughed at him. He nearly ran Mother nuts since he was always hungry. I guess it was because he had cancer. The night before we had to put him to sleep, he crawled up in my lap and as I rubbed him, he looked up at me and was trying to say, "I know what they are going to do tomorrow and it is okay, Jan, because it is for my best." I cried and I cried. We had to put him to sleep, and it nearly killed me. Mother said no more cats after that.

Dogs are not just dogs to me. They are like family. Some people do not understand that, and I can't explain it so they can understand it. I still miss Chantilly, and I guess I always will. Pets give so much love, and they do not expect anything in return. If people do not love animals, they do not understand why other people do. These dogs and cats have helped me through many a day when I did not feel well. I knew I had to hang in there, because they loved me and depended on me.

My pastor, Brother Garland Wallace, is a character and a half. He is so funny. His family planned to get a dog. Well, he didn't particularly want a dog, but he couldn't refuse this dog. So guess who in the family loves this dog more than anyone else in the family does? You guessed it. Brother Wallace does! The funny thing is that when he chewed up the family Bible. Brother Wallace said he knew he had a very religious dog. Every time he tells that story it tickles my funny bone.

Chapter 3

❖   ❖   ❖

MY GRADE SCHOOL, JUNIOR HIGH AND HIGH SCHOOL YEARS

Some people wanted me to go to a special school; however, I did not want to do so. I was stubborn and I won the victory. I started to Haskell Elementary School in 1948. All of my teachers were very good, except one. That one bad teacher was something else. Someone had written in a book and had messed the book badly. Whoever did it made it look like my handwriting, and she gave me the third degree every morning, first asking if I committed the act, then telling me I did it for sure. I had never seen the book before. I told her that, but she didn't believe me.

I admit it did look like my handwriting.. Whoever did it really did a good job of forgery. However, I still don't know how it was done. I was amazed. I told Mother I was considering make a false admission, just to get her off my back. "No you're not," Mother responded. I dreaded going to school, knowing each morning she'd drill me again. My fellow students were angered by the way she treated me, and about other things she did in the classroom. She only taught there for one year. I could see why.

All of my other teachers saw great potential in me. I was fortunate to have such good teachers. They expected only my best. Some of the students made fun of me, but Mother was wise in not making too much out of it. However, most of the students—as well as their parents-- accepted me.

How students' parents feel determines greatly whether fellow students accept you or not.. I looked forward to interaction with others each

Jan's 4th grade class, Haskell Elementary School

day. Then, at school day's end, I looked forward to being with Mama Sue, who always was eager to help me change my clothes and prepare me an afternoon snack. Invariably, she was as glad to see me as I was to see her. She was my rock. After home work was done, I'd either visit neighbors or go play with my friends.

Wednesday nights, we went to the farm to see Grandmother and Granddad, and Lightning always went us. Somehow, she always knew when Wednesdays rolled around, and was always ready to go. She'd follow us around and bark, as if urging us to begin the trip!

Occasionally, family members on both sides would come to visit. I'd always urge them to come at separate times, so we wouldn't have to spread ourselves around. Oh, well, they did care enough to visit, and we can't have everything our way. We always looked forward to visits, and they were "super big" when all gathered for Thanksgiving, Christmas, Easter and spring break. Both grandmothers were wonderful cooks, and did we ever eat well!

I spent many happy summer days at my grandparents' farm. We'd sit outside at night, looking at the stars and searching the skies for shooting stars. I also loved going to the laundry with my Mama Sue.

I always looked forward to Christmas because I knew Santa Claus was coming. I remember one Christmas when we spent Christmas with Great-Aunt Ann and Great-Uncle Arnold. I had asked for a baby's bed, and Santa Claus brought it all the way to Dallas. That always amazed me, but I admit to being among the most gullible.

I used to spend summers with Vera, Luther, Kent and Kay. We sometimes went to shows, rodeos and performances on ice. We had wonderful times together. I remember one time when a theater usher with a flashlight helped us find Kay's contact lenses. We had plenty to do, playing with our dolls, badminton and working in time for sunbathing, too.

When the time came for me to promote to Haskell Junior High School, officials advised me against it. However, those who know me best expect me to forge on, sometimes going against what is recommended. At first, I wrote by hand, then I used a manual typewriter. When the electric typewriter was invented, I got one, and I am still using it to this day. My math teacher, Mrs. Henry, was amazed how I did my math on the typewriter. I was amazed, too, but it made it so much easier on me. However, I still wrote by hand in the classroom.

My fellow students and my teachers were so interested and extremely supportive. Mr. Bell, my science teacher, was so kind and patient with me. I just loved him. It was very hard on me, but with my mother's help and the kids' help, I made it. I'd work a while on my homework, and then I would go play with the neighborhood children and my friends. I always looked forward to my mother coming home from work. Mama Sue always cooked a good supper for us. She provided constant help.

Mama Sue worked at home and took care of me while Mother worked. During holidays, when crowds came to my grandparents' house, some would stay at our house to visit Mama Sue. Hazel, Rae, Bill, Mike, and Rebecca Sue lived in Stamford, near Haskell. Rae is Mama Sue's son and my uncle. There were many visits, them to see us and vice versa. We had much fun together.

Paula Jo, also, came home on the holidays and in the summer to see both sets of her grandparents, She'd also visit Mother, Mama Sue and me, too. I especially loved Paula's Granddad and Grandmother Free.

Paula came to visit us after attending a family reunion. She said she was glad to drop by, since she was "tired of smiling." Mother and I both cracked up. Paula often misunderstood to the point of humor. One time, Mother said, "The freeze got my flowers." I wondered why Mrs. Free would want our flowers. Right away, Mother explained to Paula and me what she meant!

We loved visiting my Great-Aunt Ann and my Great-Uncle Arnold in Dallas. All through junior high in the summer, we'd visit with Vera, Luther, Kent and Kay. Mother and I would visit them on weekends, too. We also spent many hours shopping and sometimes eating out. Vera had a lot of fun teasing me.

We also went to see Cecil and Vanna Lee in Pampa and Holt and Effie in Monahans. Mother and I went to the movies often, including visit to the drive-in theater in Rule. We always took Lightning with us—she loved to go. I went to the show by myself sometimes, too. They had some really good movies back then. I miss good movies.

Sam, who worked with my mother, was a very good friend. Sometimes the three of us went to movies together, and Sam often came over to eat supper with us.

One summer, when I was in junior high, I went to Kerrville, Texas, to attend the Lions' Camp for Crippled Children. There were all ages of handicapped kids and teenagers with all kinds of handicaps. The kids were from all over the state of Texas. They had many varied activities, and I really enjoyed them. We played all kinds of games and had arts and crafts every day. They had daily canoeing, which I loved. Swimming, though, was no fun—I was scared of the water. However, I went anyway. There was also horseback riding daily, and I loved it. (I always wanted a horse of my own, but we simply couldn't afford it.) We hiked every other day, and I loved the beautiful Kerrville countryside. Counselors assigned to each participant helped us greatly with whatever we needed. As might be assumed, girls and their counselors slept in separate buildings from the boys and their leaders.

One night, it was announced we were going camping. When I heard that, my feathers fell because I never cared much for camping out. The next morning we got up early. Our overnight bags packed, we hiked for a while, then set up our camp. Of course, we had to have all kinds of help. Soon we had a campfire, and we roasted our supper. The food tasted so good. I dreaded the night ahead, however. I didn't sleep at all that night, as I knew would be the case. I lay awake, hearing all kinds of noises, including tents flapping in the wind. It was the longest night ever. I was so glad when morning came. After a wonderful breakfast, we hiked back to camp, but it was a challenge to make it through the day....

I met some really neat kids at camp, but soon it came time for us to go home. On the final night at an awards program, I won an award. Mother, Vera, and Kay came to take me home. I kept up with one cerebral palsied girl for a long while through letter exchanges. However, we finally lost contact. I'd really like to see her again one day.

When it came time for me to enter Haskell High School, again, I was advised against it. Again, I registered anyway. (Sometimes, the word "no" goes missing from my vocabulary!) Some of the people said I'd never make it, but make it I did! We had some really good teachers at Haskell High. They included Mrs. Weaver, Mrs. Couch, Mr. McCoy, Mr. Dan Smith, Mrs. Middleton, Mr. Bill Blakely, Mrs. McCollum and Mr. Gaines.

Mr. Gaines was an excellent American History teacher. I did not particularly like American History, but he made it interesting; it also turned out to be easy. We lost him during our high school years and were all sad. He was a wonderful man.

English teachers were Mrs. Weaver and Mrs. Middleton; both of them were hard. However, they taught us how to write term papers, and they really prepared us for college. I always wondered what kind of English teachers they had when they were in high school. Some of the college kids were not as educated as I was in writing term papers.

Mr. Blakely was a good math teacher. I didn't like math much, but I loved algebra. Mrs. Couch was an effective typing teacher. Even though I had been typing for years before I got into her class, she taught me much more. Mr. King was our superintendent and Mr. McCollum was principal.

Most of the boys at Haskell High were "good 'uns," but some were ornery, too. One day, during Mrs. Middleton's class, one of them asked her how many weeks until she would announce a paper assignment. Laughing, she answered, "You must have the paper in today." He knew what the answer would be when he asked the question, but hey, it didn't hurt to ask!

Overall, we had a special group of students in my class at Haskell. There will never be a finer group than the ones I graduated with. They are part of the reason I am successful today. Included were students who not only were smart, but also talented, enthusiastic and strongly committed to the work ethic.

Bobbie is a "chestnut." We have been friends since we were toddlers, and we still are friends today. She was most helpful to me when we were in school. I also ran around with Carolyn Bruce, Sandra Howard and Joy Bevel. Carolyn is a "coconut." We spent the night together, went to each other's birthday parties, went to shows and spent considerable time visiting. We played dolls one day and dressed up the next day.

One summer Vera, Luther, Mother, Kay and I went to Ruidoso, New Mexico. It was so pretty and cool up there. The pine trees smelled so good, and the mountains were gorgeous. We stayed in a cute little log cabin. We went sightseeing, and it was breathtaking. Mother, Kay and I went horseback riding. As stated earlier, I love horses. We did just fine until my horse saw some water. He nearly threw me over his head, and I could not get him to go. Our guide told me to kick him. I did, but it did no good. Disgusted with me, the guide said, "Keep on kicking him!" So I did, and the horse finally took off again. When it came time to go back to the barn, the horse really did get in gear, realizing the ride was almost over. When we got back in the car, I asked Kay and my mother, "Why is it always my horse that causes a problem?" Mother and Kay both said, "Because he knows it is you." I told them, "Shut up!" They both laughed.

We visited Ruidoso shops and bought postcards and other things. We kept our cameras busy, and saw some Indians on one of our sightseeing trips. They were selling trinkets. Mother wanted to take their pictures, but one Indian woman objected, got really mad and chased Mother down the mountain. We all got away from there in a hurry. We laughed about it later, but it wasn't funny at the time. We also visited beautiful caves, and when it was time to return home, none of us wanted to leave.

On the way back, we toured Carlsbad Caverns. They are huge! We walked part of the way down, then took the elevator to the lowest level. Then, we walked out. Thousands of bats came out at night, and that was something to see! I was glad we went, but I didn't think the caverns were all that pretty.

One summer during high school days, Vera, Luther, Mother, Kay and I toured several states. Texas itself is a big state, and it seems to take forever to reach its border. You drive for hours before you see the state line. We always had our pictures taken each time we crossed a state line. We spent the night in Oklahoma, a state I was visiting for the first time. It's a pretty state with lush grasslands. Then we drove on into Kansas, showing me where I was born. In fact, we visited the hospital in Garden City. I got to see the hospital, our apartment and where Daddy was stationed. Again, we made many pictures, then spent the night in a motel. The next morning, we toured the community, and Garden City was pretty much how I had it pictured in my mind. Its countryside is different from Oklahoma, but somehow, I believe it is the prettier state.

Then we drove into Colorado, a truly beautiful state with mountains that are majestic, colorful and simply gorgeous. They are different from the mountains of Georgia. Our destination was Tin Cup, Colorado. We traveled high up on the mountainside to get there. Vera and Luther are both characters, and they are really fun to be with, these two "butternuts." Vera fussed at Luther about his driving. I took up for him. I didn't see anything wrong with his driving. I advised him to tell her to shut up! He said, "Jan, I don't pay any attention to her." On the way up the mountainside, we all leaned to the side of the car closest to the mountain, except for Luther. Now wasn't that silly? What good would that do, if the car fell off the mountain?

We stopped to play in the snow, throwing snowballs at each other. We could see lights at the bottom of the mountain, and it surely looked like a long way down there. It was a long way down. We finally reached the small town of Tin Cup, but we couldn't see it because it was so dark outside. Luther went in to see the manager to pick up the key for our little cabin. Before unloading, we ate supper at a café in town. After unpacking, we took our baths and went to bed.

The next morning we went outside to look around. Oh! The mountains, the pine trees, the flowers and the scenery--all gorgeous! The singing birds were so pretty, and they were singing, despite it being quite cold outdoors. The food tasted so good in our cabin breakfast..

Luther loved to fish all of his life. I have never seen a man who loved to fish like he did. He fished all the time from the banks on the lakes in San Angelo. A friend had told him about a lake near the town of Tin Cup, which, if course, was one of the reasons we wanted to visit there. We could see the lake from our cabin, and he could hardly wait to get out there. He even brought his boat; it was tied on top of the car.

The lake was indeed beautiful. The water was blue and green in color and clear as glass. So, Luther went off on his all-day fishing trip, and we stayed around the cabin, eating, hiking and picking up rocks and shells. We also "drank in" the beautiful scenery. We loved every minute of it!

Luther came back to the cabin around 4 o'clock. He was a happy man. He cleaned the fish, and Vera and Mother cooked them. I have never tasted fish that good. However, sometime during the night, Luther got very sick. He was better by the next day, but when he got home he had to have a gallbladder operation. Boy! Did the operation ever make him a healthy man? He was never sick a day in his life after that. I told Mother one time if I knew it would make me that healthy, I might have the operation myself, but I never did.

The next day, we went sightseeing, again visiting some caverns. Then we went home to San Angelo, driving through some gorgeous mountain scenery, and stopping for the night at motels along the way. Mother and I stayed a few days in San Angelo, and then we drove on home to Haskell.

Lightning was sure glad to see us. She had stayed with Grandmother and Granddad Bradley.

That same summer, Mother and I took a trip by ourselves. We left Lightning with Mama Sue and traveled to Dallas to visit a few days with Great-Aunt Ann and Great-Uncle Arnold Perry. Then we drove on to the beautiful city of San Marcos, Texas, where we stayed at the La Quinta Motor Inn. The word "Aquarena" is spelled out in the sky, and it is a part of the modernistic entrance to the grounds. Heavy foliage and tall trees create a picture atmosphere for the Aquarena's diversified attractions.

We boarded the Glass Bottom Boat, and this turned out to be a thrill! We explored a silent and exotic underwater world as the electrically pro-pelled boat leisurely plied through the impressive San Marcos Springs. We sat around the edge of the boat looking down into the beautiful green, crystal water. The captain conducted an informative lecture dur-ing the journey, which lent an educational quality to the pleasure trip. We saw many beautiful fish. We saw a beautiful young woman drinking underwater. They told us that drinking underwater requires many hours of practice and training. Soda pop is replaced by air, which is forced into a bottle. Living underwater for several hours each day, Aqua-maids rival the image of legendary mermaids.

A real thrill was the scene of the huge catfish accompanied by perch, bass, and native game fish assuming unusual habits and becoming active participants of the show. We saw Missy, the swimming pig, which contra-dicts the common thought that pigs can't swim. It was an unusual sight. She also drank from a baby bottle. We also saw Glurpo, the clown, who gained national publicity for his underwater humor.

We ate at the Aquarena Restaurant. While we were eating, we viewed the beautiful fountain. Then, we walked along the walk to see many of nature's splendors. It was emphasized by the appearance of many beau-tiful swans, ducks and other fowl that enjoy their freedom throughout the grounds. We loved walking along the San Marcos River, looking at the beautiful foliage and the many gorgeous flowers. As we walked, we saw the tremendous flow of spring water gushing over the Aquarena waterfalls. Tons of clear, cool water are discharged daily by the numerous

Aquarena Springs, which flows form the beautiful San Marcos River. We even saw people fishing along the banks of this beautiful river. We could look down into the crystal clear, green water and could see fish swimming along the banks.

We rode the gondolas, used to transport passengers on the fabulous Sky Ride. The "Launching Pad" of the Sky Ride is the most architecturally unique structure designed by Texas' own famous artist-builder, Buck Winn. It looked like modern sculpture. We could look down and see fountains in the middle of the San Marcos River. The Sky Ride, which is 110 feet high above the river, leads to the beautiful Hanging Gardens. Impressive tall towers are a part of the Sky Ride installation, which affords passengers a thrill as well as a beautiful view of the countryside for miles around. The entire installation is a product of the internationally famous Von Roll factory located in Bernie, Switzerland. Swiss engineers erected the Sky Ride, and the equipment has the operating reputation of a Swiss watch.

Finally, we arrived at the beautiful Hanging Gardens, where nature, prodded by the ingenuity of man, has created another Texas wonder. We walked through nature trails full of flowering trees and shrubs. The highlight of the Hanging Gardens tour is the 100-year-old grist mill. Whole grain cornmeal is produced there in the same manner as by our forefathers of the past century.

Then, we saw the old general store and post office, where antiques are on display, and the styles of yesteryear are enjoyed in the authentic surroundings. We visited the Golden Eagle Bar, Kit Griffin Barber Shop, and The Blacksmith Shop where the past is brought into the present. Materials used in the reconstruction of this building originated from the old, historical Sam Maverick Homestead of San Antonio. Finally, we saw San Marcos' oldest house. We ate supper by candlelight in the Fountain Room of the Aquarena Restaurant overlooking the fountain. We were exhausted after a wonderful day of sightseeing, and we went back to the motel, ready for a night's rest.

The next morning, we checked out of the motel and went to breakfast. Then, we drove over to the nationally famous Summer White House of Lyndon B. Johnson. To reach it, we journeyed over the impressive Devil's Backbone Drive. Mother loved history, so she really enjoyed this. On the same property was the old rustic cabin where President Johnson was born. The Summer White House and the old rustic cabin were open to the public. The old cabin was full of old furniture from the day and time of Johnson's birth. The houses were very interesting and impressive.

Next, We drove on to Austin, Texas, to see the State Capitol and the University of Texas. The State Capitol building was most interesting. We read all of the history of the capitol; it lined the walls in printed material and pictures. We took pictures, too. We ate dinner in Austin and then drove on to the quaint little settlement of Wimberley, nestled in the Texas Hill Country. They have dude ranches and pioneer towns, providing horseback riding, swimming and fishing. We went horseback riding along beautiful trails. After we spent about two hours at Wimberley, we drove on to San Antonio, checking into the La Quinta Motor Inn before more sightseeing.

The next morning, we ate breakfast, then drove to Alamo Plaza on Houston Street. We also rode the Sky Ride over the Sunken Gardens. That was a beautiful view of some very pretty country. From there we visited the River Theater. It was a beautiful theater to view in the daytime, but I would have liked to see it at night. We just didn't have the time. From there we went to see the old and impressive Mission San Jose with a lot of history inside. Then we went on to see the famous Alamo—an impressive sight to see! I had studied about it in my history classes in school and had heard about it all my life, and about the lives that were lost in the battle waged there, but I never thought I would actually get to see it.

We went inside, and chill bumps went all over my body! We read all the history that lined the walls in picture frames, examined pictures on the walls of the famous Alamo. We toured the Alamo about an hour-and-a-half, because it took Mother so long reading everything. As I said, she loved history.

Then, we walked along the river that flows through the city of San Antonio. It has beautiful blue-green water flowing through it. From there we toured the grounds of Fort Sam Houston, where we saw the clock tower and beautiful deer roaming the grounds there. We saw the Spanish Governor's Palace and its unusual patio fountain. Then we ate dinner, resting for a while before driving toward home. Spending the night along the way, we finally arrived back in Haskell, and it was good to be home. Lightning was so glad to see us! Though we had a good trip, we were tired and hot, because we had no air-conditioning in the car.

The next summer Mother, Vera, Luther, Kay and I went back to lovely Ruidoso. We drove straight through, laughing along the way. Upon arrival, we went straight to our little cabin nestled in the pine trees. A little stream flowed beside our cabin, and the pine trees smelled heavenly! We prepared supper in our cabin, and it was wonderful. Then, it was time for bed.

The next morning after breakfast, Mother, Kay and I went horseback riding through the beautiful pine trees and the lovely mountain scenery. I was doing just fine until my horse decided to stop. Like before, it was tough getting him to go again. "Why is it always my horse that has to act up?" Mother and Kay both said, "Because he knows it is you." I said, "Well, what does that mean?" They both laughed.

Next, we went to see some Indians on their reservation. They were all dressed in native costumes. That was a fascinating sight to see. Then we went shopping, saw the old mill that is over 100 years old and toured the old Lincoln County Courthouse. The people of that area said that Billy the Kid escaped from there one time.

After lunch, we drove up to the famous Sierra Blanca Peak with its altitude of 12,003 feet, and we rode the gondolas up to the Sierra Blanca Ski Lodge, 14 miles from Ruidoso. The view was breathtaking. We took pictures, bought postcards and enjoyed a snack while taking in a beautiful view. Then, we rode the gondolas down the mountainside, stopping along the way to see the beautiful Bonito Lake. Then we saw the remarkable Monjeau Lookout -- a sightseer's paradise.

The next day, we headed for Colorado Springs. The mountains, pine trees and scenery were simply gorgeous. Some of the mountains were snow-capped. When we reached Colorado Springs, we ate lunch and then checked in at our cabin. We went sightseeing and shopping before Mother, Kay and I went horseback riding on the beautiful mountain trails.

Senior photo, Haskell High School

We visited a nearby ghost town that was bustling during the gold rush days. Back then, a lady named Baby Doe worked in a saloon there. She was married to a man who owned a mine and also had a theater in the town. Baby Doe was featured in the theater as a singer and dancer, and the men threw silver dollars at her. When the mine played out, Baby Doe and her husband refused to leave, and are said to have starved to death. What an incredible story!

The next morning, we headed for Denver. The drive from Colorado Springs to Denver was spectacular because it was covered in beautiful pine trees and mountain scenery. After checking in, there was more sightseeing and shopping, plus tours of historical sites in and around Denver that required several days.

We visited an old cemetery in the area where Billy the Kid is said to be buried. We wandered through the whole cemetery and found it to be very interesting. We also went through some caves in the area and visited other ghost towns not far from Denver. After supper that night, we went to see a show. The next morning we started our trip back to San Angelo, stopping along the way to spend the night and eat. Mother and I stayed a few days in San Angelo, then drove back to Haskell. We were tired and hot, but we were glad to be home. As usual, Lightning was especially glad to see us.

The next year was 1961, and I graduated from Haskell High School with an average of 87. I look back and wonder, "How did I do it?" Maybe it was because Mother and I stayed up every night until 10 or 11 o'clock. We were exhausted all the time. I am in better shape now than I was then. I even wore high heels then. I wish I could recall those days, but I can't. My fellow students wrote in my yearbook, "If you always keep your smile, you will always be a success in whatever you do." They were right.

We went to New Orleans on the train for our Senior Trip. We raised the money ourselves by putting on a minstrel show. We rode the bus from Haskell to Abilene to catch the train. The train was fun for all of us. We walked through the cars, visiting our friends. Mother, Mrs. Couch and Mr. King went along to keep us in line. Mr. King was a character, taking great delight in teasing me. Let's call him a "Brazil nut."

We stayed at the most beautiful hotel I had ever seen. It was three stories high, decorated all in blue and featured a lovely fountain out in the middle of the lobby with a statue in the middle of it.

Let me provide a little history of this lovely city of New Orleans. Unfortunately, one of the distinctive cities of the New World, New Orleans was established at a great cost in an environment of conflict. Its strategic position, commanding the mouth of the great Mississippi-Missouri river system, which drains the rich interior of North America, made it a pawn in the struggles of Europeans for the control of North America. As a result, its peoples evolved a unique culture and society, blending many heritages. Its citizens of African descent have provided a special contribution in making New Orleans the jazz city.

It is a city of paradox and contrast: while it shares the urban problems afflicting other U.S. cities, it has nevertheless preserved the exuberant and uninhibited spirit exemplified by its carnival season, culminating in the annual Mardi Gras, when more than 1,000,000 people take over the streets of New Orleans. The city also had a solid economic base: it is the largest city in Louisiana, the second port of the U.S. in tonnage handled, a major tourist center and a medical, industrial, and educational center.

This old-new city at the gateway of the great Mississippi Valley, brimming with romance and reminiscence of more than 200 years, merits the distinction of being called America's most interesting city. New Orleans was founded in 1718 by Jean Baptiste Le Moyne, Sieur de Bienville, and the city was christened Nouvelle-Orleans in honor of Philippe II, then regent of France under French King Louis XV. The first habitations were located along Bayou Saint John near the present city park. Adrien de Pauger, an engineer, made the French Quarter street plan and plans for the new city-to-be were laid out in 1718, taking on the appearance of a huge square, eleven blocks long and six blocks wide. The engineers charged with this task met with problems arising from uncooperative convict labors, a shortage of supplies, two severe hurricanes (in 1721 and 1722) and the unpleasant physical conditions of mosquito-infested swamps as they set up the first crude dwellings covered with bark and reeds.

In 1755, French Acadians arrived in New Orleans. The French-speaking population knew this original section of the city later as the Vieux Carre' (Old Square). The romance and the old world architecture of the beloved Vieux Carre' linger on despite the invasion of progress and modernization. In 1762 New Orleans became a Spanish Colony by the signing of the treaty of Paris. In 1767, it became capitol of Spanish Louisiana. The French Quarter was destroyed by fire twice--in 1788 and again in 1894--and 850 structures was destroyed by fire. They were rebuilt.

The Vieux Carre', or French Quarter, is a sightseer's delight. Its Creole architecture, creating the atmosphere of a foreign city, combines native architectural ingenuity with adaptations of French colonial traditions of eastern Canada and West Indian Spanish colonial styles. Typical are one-story cottages opening directly onto the sidewalks, with high-pitched roofs and windows reaching to the ground. Another style is the L-shaped, two-story dwelling with a side entrance to an inner patio. They were also built close to the sidewalk; it has a roof that extends out over balconies on both the street and patio sides. Iron grillwork, designs for which were created locally and executed to high perfection by slave craftsman, decorates these balconies and also supports the roof. Such houses are built side-by-side with no openings between them, but the patios offer space for trees, flowers, and fountains and ensure privacy for the people who live in these unusual houses. None of us had ever seen anything like these houses, and we were fascinated by them.

Central to the Veiux Carre' is Jackson Square. Part of us went to Jackson Square, one of the city's main points of interest. Jackson Square, formerly the Place d'Arms, is now a pleasant park where General Jackson sits forever on his bronze horse. Facing Jackson Square is the Old Saint Louis Cathedral, which was where the social and religious life of a land that was an empire in itself was centered. This was the most beautiful cathedral I had ever seen.

The Cabildo was, in 1800, where the colony of Louisiana was transferred from Spain to France, and where the famous Louisiana Purchase transferred the city from France to the United States in 1803. Around and beyond Jackson Square, the narrow streets and alleys wander away into the pathways of romantic history.

In wandering through these pathways to the past, we visited old and deserted corridors, as well as lovely patios and courtyards. They were made beautiful by the gorgeous and intricate iron lace balconies lining the narrow streets. From there we went to see the St. Louis Cemetery. This strange place is unique among cemeteries in that the vaults are all above ground. Then we saw a very unusual building called Lace Balconies. This lovely old building was built about 1835 by Jean LaBrance. It has beautiful iron lace balconies with intricate designs of entwined oak leaves and acorns, and is outstanding among the many buildings for which this city is famous.

We saw Brulatour Courtyard at 520 Royal Street, a lovely patio in the Vieux Carre', which is perhaps the most painted and photographed patio in the New Orleans area. The Old Absinthe House, 238 Bourbon Street, is where, according to legend, General Jackson met secretly with Jean Lafitte, the pirate-patriot, to plan the defense of New Orleans against the invading British forces. A little way down the street, we viewed the Antebelum House. They were lovely and typical Vieux Carre' residences featuring intricate iron lacework.

Along the bayou, we got to see many unique scenes in our travels to and from New Orleans. We saw the Miltenberger House, 902 Royal Street, a sturdy mansion, outstanding for its delicate lace balconies and typical fan-lighted windows. It was built in 1838. Then we walked Pirate's Alley. This narrow alley separating the Cabildo from the old St. Louis Cathedral is said to be a former haunt of colorful pirates. We stood in awe of the history of the great city of New Orleans.

The present St. Louis Cathedral completed in 1794 is the third structure erected on the same site in honor of the patron of Bourbon, France. It witnessed the exchange of flags December 1, 1803, when the flag of Spain was replaced by the tricolor of Napoleon's France, which only twenty days later was succeeded by the thirteen stars and stripes of the United States of America. We all thought we were back in that day and time. We could sense the history of the place. It made chill bumps go up and down my back.

Then, we went to see the San Francisco Plantation House. It is a sweeping structure built in 1849 of cypress and handmade brick located 28 miles above New Orleans on River Road near Reserve, Louisiana. This home preserves the spirit of the deep South, with family antiques, lovely gardens and a kindly courtesy to visitors. We all stood in awe of seeing this gorgeous structure. I had always wanted to see a southern plantation house, but I never thought I would actually get to see one. My dream came true.

The Southern Plantation House is another gorgeous house, full of lovely memories of how the old South used to be. The grounds around the house were gorgeous, too. Along the way to the house we saw the most fantastic live oak trees and many beautiful pink camellias.

Then, we went to view the Court of Two Sisters, 613 Royal Street. This building is a spacious and beautiful restaurant in a famous old townhouse in the Vieux Carre. The food was wonderful. We dined outside in this beautiful setting before returning to our hotel to rest for another day.

Next, we visited Brennan's French Restaurant, 417 Royal Street. This handsome structure and patio, one of Vieux Carre's most interesting, was erected during the twilight of the Spanish rule over Louisiana by Don Jose Faurie, a wealthy merchant. Later it housed the Louisiana Bank, the first banking institution in the Louisiana Territory. However, later still, it was the home of Paul Morphy, a world-famous chess champion. Some of us ate a snack there.

The French Market is quite a sight to see. The present site of the French Market dates back to the time of the Choctaw Indians dating back to 1791. It was destroyed by the hurricane of 1812, rebuilt a year later and remodeled in 1938. The class of 1961 thoroughly enjoyed walking through the French Market. We had never seen anything like it.

After visiting the French Market, we went into the Café Du Monde. It was a famous French Market coffee stand located near Jackson Square. Here, we enjoyed the beauties of the heart of the Vieux Carre while sipping Creole coffee and munching delicious crullers.

We surely enjoyed resting for a while and getting something unusual to eat and drink. The moss that draped oak trees and azaleas was like gray lace swinging from stately oaks along the bayous and highways of Louisiana. It is called Spanish Moss, but it is neither Spanish nor moss. It is a member of the pineapple family and it is not parasitic, as it derives its nourishment from the air.

After a short rest, we went to see the Courtyard Little Theater. It was painted pink with a beautiful fountain in the center.. Somewhere in this area, we saw a fence made in the shape of growing corn. It looked like the "real thing"—I had never seen anything like it. It was cast in 1859. After that, we were riding around and saw something else I'd never seen before. They were unbelievably beautiful trees called the Pakenham Oak Trees.

Then, we drove over the Greater New Orleans Bridge. That was quite an experience for us. This handsome structure over the Mississippi River was completed in 1958 at a cost of $60,000,000. The Bridge has a span of 1,575 feet, the largest such structure in the United States. Towering more than 350 feet above the water, its four-lanes will handle 18 million cars annually. My classmates and I enjoyed looking out over the Mississippi River.

Next, we viewed the famous Maison Montegut Courtyard. It is one of the most interesting landmarks and most beautiful patios in the Vieux Carre. The pink building with fanlight windows are Spanish-Creole architecture. The beautiful home was constructed in 1794..

Then, we visited the Bosque Courtyard and the Bosque home. This fine old mansion was erected in 1795. The home embraces this typical Spanish courtyard. It was here that Suzette Bosque, third wife of Governor Claiborne, lived. She was known as the most beautiful, fascinating and coquettish woman in New Orleans, where she was born.

From there, we drove down Royal Street with its lace balconies and Creole architecture. We saw Lafitte's blacksmith shop where, according to legend, the pirates and Jean Lafitte posed as blacksmiths and conducted their business of smuggling cargoes of "Black Gold" into the city. On our way down the street, we saw The Cabildo. This was the first administration building erected by the Spanish in the Louisiana Province. It was in this building that the Louisiana Purchase was consummated in 1803. It is now a state museum. We enjoyed learning its local history during the hour-long tour.

Starting out again the next morning, the first point of interest was Pat O'Brien's Courtyard. This ancient residence was once the townhouse of a prominent planter, Etienne Marie de Flechier, who erected it about 1792. It is now a popular refreshment establishment. Next, we saw the Spanish Courtyards with its colorful patios, and famous "Wishing Gates." It was built in 1831. We saw the most beautiful azaleas blooming in the City Park.

Then, we drove to the Mississippi River, where we rode the SS President, a spacious five-deck steamer. This modern river steamer makes a 30-mile sightseeing tour daily, providing visitors many grand views of the Port of New Orleans, the second largest port in the United States. The view from the riverbank took our breath away.

After that, we rode an old-fashioned Mississippi River stern-wheeler. This unique and interesting boat, now rarely in use, played a most important part in the development of New Orleans and the entire Mississippi Valley. I felt like I was back in the days of Mark Twain. We also went to see the Banana Dock. It was designed for the loading and unloading of banana boats.

We ate supper outside in a gorgeous setting on the patio of Brennan's French Restaurant. Don Jose Faire, a wealthy merchant, erected this handsome structure during the twilight of Spanish rule over Louisiana. We had a grand meal.

After a night's rest, we began another sightseeing day. This time, we visited the modern part of New Orleans. We rode the trolley cars up and down the street. That was quite an experience and a lot of fun. We shopped everywhere, including the stores of Stevens and Lynn's. We also went to a museum. We also went inside a beautiful motel in New Orleans called the Leonard Krower Inn.

We rode over a modern freeway to Lake Pontchartrain, a big, blue lake. We spent the rest of the day at Pontchartrain Park, a huge amusement park. Carolyn (a "coconut", remember?) and I rode the world's tallest roller coaster.

I think Carolyn and I were both nuts. We rode other kinds of rides, too. We also saw the Lake Pontchartrain Causeway. It is the world's largest bridge (23.83 miles), connecting New Orleans with the highlands to the north. It was completed in 1956, at a cost of $51,000,000, as part of the Greater New Orleans Expressway System. Eight miles of the bridge are out of sight of land. We also saw the Huey P. Long Bridge. At the end of the day, we were all tired.

The next morning was our free day, and most of us rested. That night part of us went to a fancy nightclub. We had our pictures made, saw a fancy show and I ordered champagne! I didn't drink it, though, because I didn't like the taste. Mr. King teased me about it. Mr. King said, "I think if you ordered it, you ought to drink it." The next day we came home on the train. It was a fun trip!

The summer after I graduated, Mother, Vera, Kay and I went to the newly- opened Six Flags Over Texas. We stayed in the brand new Six Flags Inn. During its history, six flags have flown over Texas. They are the flags of the Republic of Texas, Confederate, Mexico, France, Spain, and, of course, the United States of America. They looked so pretty all lit up at night. It made me feel so proud.

Let me provide some brief history of Texas. The rich heritage of Texas' colorful past and the exciting promise of her future came vividly to life at Six Flags Over Texas. For more than 115 years, except for a brief interlude of the Confederacy, Texas and the nation have marched side-by-side in the vanguard of human freedom and progress. From the epochs long past, the glory of Texas under the flags of the six sovereign nations are reborn. A new breath of life was returned by the Conquistadors, mighty soldier of Imperial Spain, to their adventures in Texas. Commanded by Francisco Coronado, the armed columns of conquerors, clad in almost medieval splendor with shining armor and plumed helmets, pursued the dancing mirages of the fabled cities of Quivira and the fabulous cities of Cibola.

The heritage of the French began in 1685 when the golden *fleur-de-lis* of France, royal standard of the grand Monarch Louis the XIV himself, was planted on Texas soil by the explorer-adventure Rene Robert Cavalier, Sieur de La Salle. Their perilous journey in 25-foot longboats up the Lavaca River against desperate odds is indelibly etched in the visitor's memory. The journey was very fascinating to us.

The bright red, white, and green Banner of Mexico flew over Texas from 1821 until 1836. Here, newcomers from the United States found a way of life blended from that of two ancient peoples—the proud Aztecs and the adventurous, fun-loving sons and daughters of Old Spain, who brought a Latin spirit to the New World.

Texans looked to the Stars and Bars of the Confederacy as their own flag during four imperishable years, 1861-1865. They remember the great struggle of a century earlier that tested the mettle of men who wore the gray and those who loved the blue, and the millions of their loved ones on each side who pledged their faith in them for a bloody civil war that pitted brother against brother.

The great days of the Old West are evoked anew in the wild and wooded era of the Republic of Texas. Its Lone Star flag reigned supreme for nine years. Perils of the frontier took shape as outlaws battled the forces of law and order, and pioneers moved ever westward, soon followed by the iron horse chugging along on a narrow-gauge railway. We rode the iron horse, and it made us feel like we were back in another century.

And so, from the coming of the Conquistadors, men looked upon the land of Texas only as a land of gold and treasure. It remained for later men to discover Quivira, not as a land of gold and treasure as envisioned by the Conquistadors, but a land offering more in natural resources than the Spanish ever dreamed of.

We went to the Mexican section of Six Flags, where geometric patterns of multicolored lighting effects reveal a fascinating and beautiful picture of the Canopied Garden Walkway leading into this section. We rode the Cha-Cha-Choo-Choo, a Fiesta Train. It embarked on an amusing journey around the Mexican countryside. As the musical train went merrily on its rails, we saw an amusing panorama of Mexico, which came to life in delightful animation. We saw dancing tamales, one of the most popular of the many colorful and comical animations on the Fiesta Train ride. This group of dancing tamales performed to the festive strains of Mexican music that filled the air.

Next, we saw the colorful animated Mexican characters lend a contagious holiday spirit to Texas' exciting new entertainment center. In the Mexican Section, sights and sounds of the mariachi band played with dark-eyed senoritas and their Caballeros dancing the Tapatio and other Mexican dances. Street markets and quaint bazaars crowded with wares of serape weavers, basket makers, and silversmiths and other master craftsmen were all around us. We saw the cool verdure and blazing color of flowers in the floating garden of Xochmilcho. Last, we saw the strolling musicians playing beautiful Mexican music. Happy are the memories that long linger after a visit to this corner of Old Mexico.

Then, we saw the Indian Village as we approached the Historic Texas Section. The Indian Village dancers danced a welcome for visitors to their village. They were dressed in typical Indian costumes. Then, we relived the days of gas footlights and greasepaint as we enjoyed an old-fashioned songfest in the Crazy Horse Saloon. It was fun to watch a "hoss" thief apprehended in the Texas Section as the sheriff of Six Flags marched the ornery critter to jail. "His trial begins tomorrow with Judge Roy Bean presiding," the sheriff told us. Then, we saw a shoot-out, and Judge Roy Bean, standing on the courthouse steps, might as well have put the hanging rope away, because the bank robber finally bit the dust under the hail of bullets from the guns of the Six Flags sheriff and his deputies.

Over by the small-town depot, we were drawn to the smoke belching from the gleaming smokestack of the Iron Horse, the powerful little steam engine ready to take us on its train of cars on one of the world's few remaining narrow-gauge railroads. Part of the train ride took us through Indian country. The painted warriors shot arrows at the train roaring through their hunting grounds. They told us it is a lucky run if the train manages to pass through this country, without feeling the flint edge of arrows against its sides or the rude halt ordered by desperadoes intent on robbing express cars and passengers. We saw quick-draw poker along the streets.

Then, we experienced a peaceful morning in the Texas section. Everything appeared calm and serene at the moment as the cowpokes passed the time of day at the general store. But look out! The action could start at any moment. We crossed the bridge to see the Doggie Hotel. The Doggie Hotel helped us relive the colorful days of Wild West Texas, where beds were 25 cents and meals were extra. Last, we saw the famous Boot Hill. After that, Mother, Kay and I rode the roller coaster and the water roller coaster. They were "fun" rides, but we got wet!

Next, we visited the Confederate section where the Old South lives again, and in the distance, a formation of men in gray could be seen marching back into town. We could see a Southern Plantation home in the distance and heard a band marching and playing the song "Dixie." You enter this section just as the urgency of war calls for volunteers for Confederacy, but peacetime ways in the old South were not yet lost. We rode the Butterfield Overland Mail Line. That was a fun-filled experience.

The man riding shotgun must be an expert, for there was no telling when outlaws or Indians would decide to stage a hold-up.

Then came our trip to Skull Island, where Jean Lafitte is said to have buried a king's ransom somewhere on the island. Today, an even greater treasure is the Swamp Tree on the island, a 30-foot-high adventure. Mother, Kay and I slid down it. That was fun! From there we went to the big amphitheater, where we enjoyed entertaining performances. We heard a live Dixieland Band playing tunes of the days straight from the heart of Dixie.

From there, we went to the French section on an exotic trip by riverboat through steaming jungles packed with danger. From the deck of the 25-foot longboat, the golden flag of France of two centuries ago fluttered from it mast. Commanding the boat was the adventurer Rene Robert Cavalier, Sieur de La Salle. Unknown hazards lay ahead along the Lavaca River. It began on the day of July 24, 1684, when four shiploads of soldiers and colonists watched as the wind swelled the sails and the expedition pulled away from the harbor of Rochfort in France. Its goal was to colonize around the mouth of the Mississippi and thus control the southern half of the continent. They sighted land at last, but it was Texas. There, they raised the flag of France challenging Spain's hold over Texas, and built Fort Saint Louis. We saw the replica of Fort Saint Louis, which had been built at Six Flags. We felt as if we were back in that day and time. Then we rode the Airlift over Six Flags, and next we ate at one of the snack areas.

Next, we went to the Spanish section. Francisco Vasquez de Coronado, greatest of the Spanish Conquistadors, led his column of adventures on a pack mule train across the landscape of the Southwest in pursuit of the phantom riches of the Seven Cities of Cibola. Here in the Spanish section, we rode the pack mule with him as he descended into Palo Duro Canyon. Indians resented the intrusion of the men on their land, and Coronado's soldiers never knew when an attack by the Indians might be launched against them. Some half a century later, they built the first mission in Texas. We saw the ruins of the church that had been restored in this section. Then, we rode the train that goes all around Six Flags.

Last, we saw the USA section. In this section, the greatest of our Common Land was shown, together with its exciting prospects as the

U.S. moves into the Space Age. Technology is here to spur even greater achievements. Symbolizing that spirit is the magnificent Astrolift. We went to find Humble's Happy Motoring Freeway, and Kay and I drove the little gasoline-powered cars along the freeways of tomorrow. Since then, we have been to Six Flags Over Texas many times. It has grown and improved so much over the years.

One summer after Mother retired, we rented a cabin for a month in Ruidoso. We had a wonderful time, doing lots of shopping and sightseeing. Cecil and Vanna Lee came up and stayed with us. We enjoyed their visit. Bill, Billie Nell and the boys were living up there at the time. We went to the horse races, where we saw lots of Haskell area people. I think I counted 101 visitors from Haskell and nearby during the month we were there, and it was a joy to see everyone..

Bill and Billie Nell took us to see a beautiful mountain nearby. We rode a sky lift, and the boys played with ladybugs. One day, Mother, Ross, Rae and I went horseback riding up this steep mountainside trail. One of the boys asked me, "Don't it scare you to look down?" I said, "Yes, it does, so let's don't look down."

When we got back down to the bottom of the mountain, Mother and I had trouble standing up. Our legs wouldn't hold us up. Finally, we managed to stand up by ourselves. It was a frightening feeling. The guide was not much help. Bill and Billie Nell thought it was funny. Another time, Bill and Billie Nell were going on a trip, so they invited us to "house sit" for them and feed their dogs. They lived in an A-framed cabin. We loved the smell of the pine trees. We sure enjoyed that. We didn't want to come back to hot and dry Texas.

My Haskell High School classmates still get together at HHS Homecomings. We have as many as 60 people at almost every class reunion. All of my classmates have senses of humor, and we have so much fun laughing and talking old times. We lost Ben Anderson to a heart attack and we've also lost James Cameron and Sandra Howard. Carroll Macon puts out a newsletter occasionally, keeping everyone updated on each other. Classmates send in letters to him about what is going on in their lives. This has been going on for a long time now. Isn't that neat?

Chapter 4

❖　❖　❖

COLLEGE YEARS, WITH A VARIETY OF ASSORTED NUTS

After high school, I wanted to go to college, and here again, I was told it would be impossible for me to go. I'd heard that before, and plowed on. I enrolled at Hardin-Simmons University in the fall of 1961. I was a dorm resident for the first five years. The girls there were so sweet to me and would do anything for me. I so enjoyed my dorm years at HSU.

My freshman year, Janet was my roommate. She was wonderful and so helpful, assisted me in getting dressed, undressing and in dozens of other ways. The best thing that ever happened was when they started making pants with elastic in them. Janet, who tried to hold down too many jobs, was also the school nurse. Sadly, she had a nervous breakdown, leaving HSU during my sophomore year. Though I'd love to, I never heard from her again. Since I have so much trouble sleeping, I never had another roommate, but did have two suite mates during subsequent years. Two dorm mothers also provided much assistance. They were named Miss Culpepper and Mrs. Hicks. Miss Culpepper had a wonderful sense of humor. These dorm mothers were strict, but they were really good with their girls.

After my first year, I got really sick. Hopefully, I'll never be that sick again. It was horrible! Mother took me to see Dr. Beal, an Abilene neurologist. He was a very smart doctor who had suffered a nervous breakdown himself. I've always believed this deepened his understanding of

James Cogburn, Abilene
Kathy Colgan, Megargel
Janet Conradt, Blackwell
Kathy Cotton, Breckenridge
Philip Craik, Abilene

Glen Crosthwait, Olney
Dana Davis, Dallas
David Dean, Abilene
Collette DeFrey, Abilene
Jim Dermody, Abilene

Jan Eastland, Haskell
Bill Ellis, Abilene
Cecil Evans, Carlsbad, N.M.
Margaret Evans, Crystal City
Randy Fout, Boise, Idaho

Suzanne Fox, Abilene
Israel Garcia, Wichita, Kansas
Marsha Gould, Talpa
Baldemar Gutierrez, Abilene
Phyllis Harbin, El Paso

Linda Harris, Abilene
Jo Elaine Hatton, Dallas
Melba Hernandez, Ft. Worth
Pam Hicks, Dallas
Susan Hill, Abilene

Patricia Hogan, Abilene
Robert Halcomb, Odessa
David Holland, Englewood, Colo.
Annette Howard, Lubbock
Scot Howard, Abilene

HSU 1974 *BRONCO*

52

patients' problems. I described my symptoms to him, and he responded immediately, correctly diagnosing what was wrong with me.

Dr. Beal said my body chemistry was out of balance, and I was depressed. He started me on Elavil, and I got better immediately. I could not believe I felt better so quickly. When he took me off the medication, I'd get sick again, then have to drop out of school for a while before returning.

He also prescribed a sleeping pill that made decent sleep possible for the first time in my life.

Finally after taking me off medication twice, Dr. Beal told my mother, "I guess we are just going to have to leave Jan on the meds." He didn't want me to be addicted, but I have been fine ever since.

Men with cerebral palsy don't seem to have as much problem sleeping as do cerebral palsied females. The pill made my coordination better and my speech better, too. I cannot explain it. The name of the medication was Elavil. I have had many people who had seen me before and after the treatment, including Mr. Shelley Smith, ask me what I had done to make myself better and into a new person. It was such a drastic change, and it was almost unbelievable. I think it was a miracle from God.

There were many times that I did not think I could graduate from HSU, but the many wonderful people of Haskell encouraged me to stay the course. What they would say to help me more than anything else was, "Hang in there Jan, you sure have helped me." I would read *Guideposts* and read what others had to overcome, and their stories would encourage me. I have never been treated better than I was at HSU—except for the people in my hometown of Haskell.

I still keep in touch with some of my friends I first met at HSU. Those were my happiest days. I told my professors I wanted to major in sociology and minor in psychology. But, here again, I was told it would be impossible to major and minor in two such difficult subjects. However, after they saw how determined I was to do it, they soon learned I was up to the challenge.

Dr. Lunday and Mr. Osborne were my first professors in sociology, and Dr. and Mrs. Ford were my first professors in psychology. After Dr. Lunday and Mr. Osborne retired, another sociology teacher took their place. Dr. Greenfield was a very good sociology teacher. I made B's in his class. He was the first professor to really encourage me in my field. The reason he did was he went to Seminary with some people who were afflicted with cerebral palsy, so he knew what they had done.

When I could no longer afford to stay in the dormitory, I commuted with other ladies from Haskell who also were attending HSU. Some of them were Billie, Gerri, Betty and Martha. We had lots of fun talking and laughing. Some of them were silly and nutty.

Martha and I had a lot of fun together. She is a "pistachio nut." We stopped at a drive-in to get something to drink and saw a man standing outside with a monkey wearing a disposable diaper and sitting on his shoulder. Martha said to me "Do you see what I see?" I said, "I am afraid I do." We both started laughing.

One time I told Martha about how my aunt doesn't know a joke. Some people just don't understand joking. They are so serious minded that I almost feel sorry for them. Then I told Martha that my aunt wouldn't know a joke if it flew up and hit her in the face. Martha started laughing her head off. Martha and I were coming home one day, and we saw a house sitting in the middle of the highway, and we had to go around it. Martha and I both said, "They will never believe us in Haskell!" We both started laughing again. We had lots of fun driving back and forth going to class. I told another friend named Joel that I felt that like a yo-yo, and he broke into laughter.

During my commuting days, I did some babysitting in my hometown. I was sitting with the cutest little redheaded boy you ever saw. His name was Henry, and Henry said that I was the best babysitter in town, because I played with him. He thought I was about his age. I saw him years later at a wedding at my church in Abilene. My preacher's son married the girl who lived in our house after we moved away. I got to meet his wife and nieces. We sat down at the reception and talked a while. Henry told me the sweetest thing. Henry said, "You have given me some beautiful memories." What he said to me made me feel very happy. I also got to see James, his older brother.

I love children, but I can't have them. So I go around adopting them. Some of my children lived next door to me in Haskell. Their names were Mark, James, Joseph and Patrick. Mark was the oldest. He gave me a gift one time with a note attached to it that said, "To the sweetest neighbor I have ever had." Wasn't that sweet of him?

James accidentally broke a window in our house. He had to say that he did it. One time I told Joseph that he was cute. Joseph said that he knew it. Joseph was a very hyper child. He was so hyper that he could not sit still. One day, I was over at their house, and Mary Nell said to Gerald, "What are we going to do with him?" Gerald looked at her and grinned and said, "We are going to keep him." I laughed and I laughed. Gerald spanked his boys out in the backyard. I knew they needed it, but I couldn't stand to hear them cry, so I went into my house. Their daddy, Gerald, loved to tease me. Gerald is so ornery, until he hurts. He is another nut, but I have not figured out what kind of nut he is. I guess he is another "peanut."

Then, I lived near four girls. They were also fun to be with. Their names are Kim, Kay, Kathy and Kristin. They were and are sweet girls. They are all grown and married and have children of their own now.

I started working in the HSU Post Office in 1965, and I worked there until I graduated. I still continued to drive back and forth and go to school and worked there. I sure had fun. I sure enjoyed putting up the mail. Every one of my bosses were so sweet and helpful, especially Mr. Gerald Armstrong. My bosses -- as well as fellow students -- loved to pick on me. I do not know what it is about me that make people tease me. That is their favorite pastime.

There was a postman from Hamlin, and I was from Haskell. He started teasing me about Hamlin beating Haskell in football. Then he started teasing me about a Chinaman being my boyfriend. Now why a Chinaman, I will never know! He does not know it, but he really started something, and it is still going on to this very day. I could kill him. Every time he brought the mail, he would say something about the Chinaman and me. I would tell him "Shut Up" and he would laugh and laugh.

My bosses and the rest picked up on it, especially Ronda, who was a "butternut." One summer, she nearly ran me nuts. By that time the postman had quit coming to deliver the mail, and another postman was coming. I told her that I was going to start writing down everything that she said to me and go to Hollywood and become a comedy writer. She could think of more things to say about the Chinaman and me. I think she stayed up nights trying to think of things to say to me. I also told her that she was going to drive me nuts, and I would end up in the mental hospital. Ronda said that it would not do me any good, because she would just follow me up there. Ronda was big and fat and every ounce of her was pure-D orneriness.

The professors heard about it and picked up on it, too. They would holler at me through the mailboxes. They all had more fun. I told them all to "Shut Up!" I also told them that it was a good thing I had a sense of humor, because if I didn't, there would be a bunch of dead people lying around HSU. Ronda told her friends about it, and they started teasing me, too. One day my boss, Mr. Armstrong, told me that I was wanted on the phone. I could not imagine who it was. I went to the phone, and there was some boy talking in Chinese, and he wanted to take me out to eat at a Chinese restaurant, but before I could say, "Yes," the boy hung up. I told Gerald, my boss, "Well, you'll never guess who that was." I told him about it, and he sure did laugh. I told him that I was going to make out like I never got that phone call. I knew Ronda had put someone up to doing it, and I knew it would spoil her fun.

It was Friday, and I didn't think I would see her again until Monday. However, mother picked me up, and we went to McDonald's to eat lunch. I looked up and there was Ronda as big as life itself. She came up to me, and Ronda said, "I heard that you got a phone call." I looked at her with a straight face and said, "What phone call? I didn't get a phone call!" She had the funniest look on her face. I would not have taken a million dollars for a picture of that look on her face. I denied getting that phone call for weeks. It broke her heart, but I thought it was extremely funny.

About three weeks later, I said, "Yes, Ronda, I got that darn phone call." That really made her day. I found out later who made the phone call. It was my preacher's son from Haskell. I told him I could kill him. He would see me on campus, and he would say, "A'so! A'so! Honorable Jan." Everyone would look at us like we were nuts. I would tell him to "Shut Up," but it didn't do any good. So one day he said, "A'so! A'so!" and I said, "A'chew! A'chew!" I told the people in Haskell about it, and they sure thought it was funny.

I told some of my friends that Ronda was about to drive me nuts, and they said, "Do something to her!" So Mother and I wrote on her car window in red lipstick, "The Chinaman has been here! The ABC Bombers are watching you." Do you know it made her mad? I could not believe it. She could dish it out, but she couldn't take it.

Ronda said that she was going to send the police after me for malicious mischief. I said, "What do you think you have been doing to me?" We have all graduated, and they are still teasing me about that darn Chinaman. I could kill that postman from Hamlin, because he has no idea what he started.

John went back to California to live and work. Bobby moved to the Dallas-Fort Worth area, and works for Southwestern Bell Telephone Company. Ronda is still in Abilene as far as I know. Bobby goes to see John from time to time. They went to Chinatown in California and called me long distance. They were eating at a Chinese Restaurant. Bobby and John said, "They wished I was there." I told them both to Shut Up! They have called me several times from Chinatown, and sent me a Chinese newspaper with my name on it. They sent me a Chinese-looking cup, as well as a Chinese Christmas card.

Just recently they called me, laughing up a storm. Bobby and John said, "You will not believe this, but we found a Jan's Chinese eating place in Chinatown in California." They were laughing so hard they couldn't talk. They even sent me a menu.

One time they came to Abilene and took me out to eat at the China Hut. It was my birthday, and they had the waiters sing "Happy Birthday" to me in Chinese. How they pulled that off, I will never know. Just recently, they sent me another Chinese newspaper. I can't even read Chinese, of course. Since then, they sent me an Elvis Presley impersonator's scarf. Every time I see certain professors out in town, they still ask me if I have been eating at a Chinese restaurant. Dr. Aston is one of them. I just tell them all, "Shut Up!"

Nobody can say "Shut Up!" like I can, since I have had lots of experience. One day while I was at work, my boss and co-workers practiced trying to say "Shut Up!" the way I do, but they couldn't. They told me later that they think when I die and go to heaven, I'll have slanted eyes, and will be assigned to the Chinese section there.

John, the "ginkgo nut," was a Jew who went to a Baptist University. Then he became a Catholic priest. Now how about that! Elvis Presley was coming to Abilene, and I wanted to go see him. So I asked John to take me. John could see how excited I was. I had been a fan of Elvis Presley since I was a teenager, but never expected ever to see him in person. By the time I saw him, he was so doped up that he looked terrible. I always thought it was such a shame what they did to him. He couldn't handle his fame, and he had people around who were not his real friends. I also thought it was a shame what he did to his wife, Priscilla, and his daughter. Lisa begged him to get off drugs, but by that time, he was so addicted he couldn't. I was still his fan until he died because I felt sorry for him. He could really sing good gospel music. He really was a very talented person.

I also was privileged to see Jerry Lee Lewis in concert.

When I was working in the HSU Post Office, a professor, Dr. Zane Mason, taught history. Dr. Mason is a "pinion nut." He liked to tease me about junk mail. Dr. Mason said that it was all my fault, and I said it was not my fault. We had more fun. He also liked to tease his other students. One day, he came upon one of his students talking to his girlfriend. Dr. Mason asked the boy, "Is this the crossed-eyed girl that you were telling me about?" The girl, Carol, turned to her boyfriend and said, "Did you tell him I was cross-eyed?" I wish I could have seen the expression on that boy's face.

As I said, Dr. Mason liked to tease me about junk mail. Dr. Mason would say, "You just put junk mail in my box on purpose." I said, "No, I don't!" So I went home and got my junk mail put it in his box. He gave me a hard look and kept on teasing me. From then on I put everything in his box. I put a brick in his box from an old building being torn down. He thought that was funny. I got a baby's toy apple with a bell on it and put it in his box. I asked him later what he did with it, and Dr.

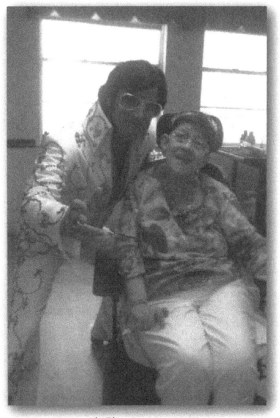

Jan with Elvis impersonator at Coronado Nursing Center in 2009

Mason said he hung it over his bed and played with it every night before he went to sleep. Also, he drank a cup of hot water every day at lunch, so I put a cup of hot water in his post office box. He sure thought that was funny. I sure miss him and all the fun we had. Even though he was a professor and I was a student, we had a special friendship. We respected each other, and he sent me the following letter, and it meant the world to me.

December 18,1975
Miss Jan Eastland
244 N. Willis, Apt. 141
Abilene, Texas 79603

Dear Jan,

Just a line to tell you I wish for a most happy Christmas time. It has been my privilege to know you through these years and to have the opportunity to sit down often and talk with you. I am deeply appreciative of the "apple," etc. for the they remind me of you and the attributes of your life. You are so loved on this campus and you have so many friends and I know that you are aware of this. May our dear Lord hallow these present days for you and yours and bring you your heart's desire. May His grace provide all of your needs and keep you always looking up...after all, He could come for us one of these days and we must be looking for Him.

My devotion,
Zane A. Mason
Professor of History

I met a girl named Dolores while at HSU who worked in the cafeteria. She was sweet, but she was also ornery. I loved her, and still do to this day. She made a dress for me and sewed the pockets on upside down. She was not going to change them either, and she got mad at me for getting someone else to change them. I said, "Dolores, if you think that I am going to wear this dress in public with pockets sewed upside down, you are crazy."

We both met a wonderful boy named Terry. He is the sweetest boy, but he is silly, too. We three ran around together, and we had a lot of fun. Dolores and Terry are both "hickory nuts," because I met them on Hickory Street in Abilene. Dolores did not study, and she tried to get me not to study. I told her that I was there to study. She came to HSU to find herself a husband. She put cheese on my nose one day. It made me mad, so I squirted cheese all over her mirror in her dorm room. She had difficulty getting the cheese off her mirror. Dolores said, "Why did you do that?" said, "Do you really have to ask?" We went to the park one day, and she got me on the seesaw, refusing to let me down. I fell off, and she just sat there and laughed at me. She is some friend. She gets the craziest cards and sends them to me, and she wrote letters to me in a circle or in shorthand. I cannot even read shorthand.

Terry, Dolores and I -- along with some more friends -- went on a picnic at a local park and got into a watermelon fight. I came into the dorm lobby with red and orange stains all over my clothes. My dorm mother asked me, "What happened to you?" I said, "You will not believe it," and pointed to Dolores.

One time, I went with them to an HSU rodeo. I ought to have known better. I followed them, and they had no idea where they were going. I was stupid, because I followed them. We ended up in a corral with a bunch of wild horses running around. We could have been killed. We had to climb under a fence in order to get to the rodeo. I told Dolores and Terry, "I am not crawling under that darn fence. Do you think I am crazy?" I have never crawled under a fence in my entire life. Terry and Dolores said, "Do you want to go back through all those horses?" I said, "No! I don't!" Well, halfway under that darn fence, Marshall Walker, head of the Baptist Student Union, asked me, "Jan, what in the world are you doing?" I said, "What does it look like I am doing. I'm trying to get under this darn fence." They all laughed. I said to Dolores and Terry, "Now look what you all have done to me. You have ruined my reputation. He probably thinks I didn't pay to get in."

Well, Terry and Dolores fell in love. They were just made for each other. Neither of them had any sense. They were going to get married, and they wanted me to be their maid of honor. I said, "No way!" Dolores and Terry said, "All right, we'll just not get married." I said "That is blackmail!" So I finally agreed to be their maid of honor. I must have been nuts. On the way to the wedding, we stayed in motel in Graham, Texas.

Dolores' mother was the cutest and sweetest thing. She had made signs and put them along the road, so we could find their house out in the country. I told Dolores' mother, "Now I know where Dolores got her orneriness, and her love for having fun." Her mother told me later that she would never forget that.

Dolores' father was a Baptist preacher. He was a very fine man, and he performed the wedding. He put Terry's ring on my thumb, because I was holding her bouquet. I told him it wouldn't work, but he said it would. He said, "I am going to say a few more words, before we get on with the wedding." Well, he said more than a few words. I thought he was never going to stop talking—he preached a sermon. Finally, it was time for us to go in. I got up there okay, and so did the other girls, but when Dolores tried to step up, she tripped on her wedding gown. Someone laughed out loud in the back of the church. I did not even start laughing, because I knew if I did, I was so nervous I would not stop, and I would probably wet my underwear.

Well, everything went all right until her daddy, Brother Lyons, tried to get the ring off my thumb. He almost didn't get it off. The more he tried, the more nervous he got. Mother asked me later, "What was Brother Lyons doing all that time?" I told her he was trying to get the ring off my thumb. I sure am glad that he finally did, because I didn't want to be the one that ended up getting married. The candles were hot. I thought I was going to faint. They sang the funniest song at the end of the wedding. I had never heard that song at a wedding before in my life. They sang *God Be With You Till We Meet Again*. The piano player got the song mixed up with another song, and Dolores was too nutty to tell him. It was a sweet wedding, but I never intend to do that again. I was a nervous wreck. I am not even going to be in my own wedding. I was more nervous than Dolores was. It was on Valentine's Daye I will never forget!

Dolores, Terry and I are still friends. I went to visit them shortly before the birth of their first child. I woke up early one morning and decided to go outside. It was a beautiful morning. I stayed outside about fifteen minutes and decided to go back inside, but I discovered that I had accidentally locked myself out of the house. It was six o'clock in the morning. I knew Dolores would kill me if I woke her up that early in the morning. I waited until eight o'clock, and then I woke them both up standing looking in their bedroom window. I looked stupid, and I felt stupid. Dolores said,

"What in the world are you doing outside at this time of the morning?" I told her what I had done! She will never forget it either.

Once, their plumbing stopped up from tree roots, but they blamed it on me. They were teasing, of course. We had to go to the church to use the bathroom! They were having a revival at the time (I gave my testimony). Dolores told me later that she saw the preacher who preached the revival in Fort Worth, and he asked her, "How is the girl who stopped up your plumbing?" She told him that I was all right. What a way to be remembered!

After that, we went to see them once a year and had dinner with them. Their children's names are Hallie, Fern and Jessie. They are all grown and married now and have children of their own. They mean a lot to me. Dolores' daddy died suddenly. We surely did miss him. He was a fine man. Dolores' mother died of cancer a while back. I sure miss her, too, and all the good times we had together. I really loved Dolores' mother, and she was a precious person. I never knew Terry's family very well, because they lived so far away. However, I would have loved them, too, if I had a chance to get to know them.

One time, Dolores and her children came to see us, and we went to the show. I told them to buy their drinks before we went in since they are so expensive if you buy them at the theater, but they would not let us take them in, so Dolores had to drink hers down real fast. She could not enjoy the show, because she was so full. Dolores said, "Wouldn't you know Jan would pull something like that on me!" I was innocent, because I was just trying to help them save money.

She sent me a crazy chain letter one time, and I had more fun showing it to everyone. She and her children helped us celebrate one of Mother's birthdays at home. We had a birthday cake and everything. We were trying to decide what we were going to eat, and I recalled that Mother and I had eaten some good fried chicken at one of the pizza places here in town. They told us we would have to order it from home. Now isn't that stupid! Dolores said, "Are you sure you live in this town? You do not seem to know what is going on." I told her to Shut Up! Dolores said that she could not wait to get home to tell Terry what I had done.

A good many years ago, Terry was out of a job and discouraged, so I took them out to eat at the Royal Inn. I prayed for them, and he found a better job. Dolores used to work at the local post office. Dolores sent me a crazy T-shirt that she made on her computer. The T-shirt had the words written on the front of it that said, "People with Cerebral Palsy are not retarded," but on the back of the T-shirt, it said, "They get a little crazy sometimes." It also had a crazy-looking woman on the back of it. She thought I was crazy, because I moved in with people who stole my money. And I wear the shirt, and every time I wear it, people think it is funny. A friend of hers asked her, "Are you really going to send that shirt to Jan?" Dolores said, "Yes, I sure am!" I am telling you, if I can pick some nuts as friends, but I love them so.

Chapter 5

❖   ❖   ❖

HARDIN-SIMMONS YEARS, PHASE TWO

I was continuing my education at HSU when I found a lump in my breast. It was removed, and I feared it to be cancer, of course.

However, the night before entering the hospital, I asked Dr. Cadenhead if he would pierce my ears while I was sedated. He and his wife convulsed in laughter; a serious moment was lightened.

When the surgery began, I remember hearing Dr. Colbert asking Dr. Cadenhead: "What in the world are you doing?" His answer: "Getting ready to pierce this girl's ears." Upon awakening, I felt of my newly-pierced ears! The whole hospital got a big bang out of it!

Soon, I asked Dr. Cadenhead how long I'd be in the hospital. "Two weeks," he answered. "Oh, it's not the surgery -- it's your ears!"

I told him to Shut Up!" He left my room, laughing and I was home in three days!

Before entering HSU and during my time there, Haskell High School had its homecoming every two years. There has always been a large group of our close-knit classmates. Carol Macon provides updates on what is going on in classmates' lives, as well as current contact information. Often, I attended my mother's 1929 class reunion as well. It started in 1939, and is held all over Texas, kept going largely by the efforts of John English, who is now deceased. Since his death, we've missed reunions of this "depression bunch." They somehow scraped together funds to provide me with two scholarships to HSU. They loved me and I loved them.

I enjoyed going with Mother to her homecomings; we'd always get together at someone's house. I grew up knowing many of her classmates. Around 1964, I went with Mother to Ira Hester's house for the class party. I enjoyed their animated visits.

Once I saw a handsome man in fine-looking clothes in the mix; I'd never seen him before. Mother told me he was Charles Bates Thornton, a multi-millionaire who graduated from HHS in 1931.

Years later, while enjoying a coke in Oates Drugstore, I saw him again. After introducing myself to him, I inquired what brought him back to Haskell this time. It was for his step-father's funeral.

At another homecoming, Mr. Thornton phoned my mother, asking my whereabouts. I was helping my precious friend Sherry round up refreshments for our class party that night. Mother wondered why he asked specifically about me, so I told her the story of meeting him in the drugstore.

Since he was coming by later, Mother put up her ironing board and straightened the house. Flora, Mr. Thornton's beautiful wife, was from Fort Worth, and that's where he left her when visited Hamlin. I so wish she would have accompanied him just once. I would have loved to meet her.

When he came by the house, I introduced him to Sherry. I was wide-eyed that he'd brought gifts, including a portable typewriter with a radio in it, a solid gold pen and pencil set and a copy of his book, *Someone Has To Make It Happen*. I went into orbit! He wanted me to write to him in California and keep him updated on my college work.

I was so excited I forgot to ask him to autograph my book. Thankfully, he had already done so. I could not believe this was really happening to me. I pinched myself to see if I was dreaming. Bates was such a compassionate person. I saw him again at the program Saturday afternoon and that night at the Country Club party, after the 1961 class reunion party at my house. The party at the County Club was for everyone, so I got to see him again.

Then on Sunday, Bates flew back to California in his jet plane.

Jan with American business executive, founder of Litton Industries and 1931 Haskell High School graduate, Charles Bates Thornton. Thornton took a special interest in Jan and encouraged her in many ways.

Mother thought I would never come down to earth, because weeks after homecoming was over, I was still on cloud nine. I wrote him a "thank you" letter, and he wrote me back. I could not believe a man as busy as he would write me letters. He surely helped lifting up my ego. Here's one of his letters:

November 20, 1969
Dear Jan,
    What a pleasant surprise when I returned to the office today from a business trip in New York City and found your nice letter dated November 16, 1969.
    I, too, enjoyed the Homecoming activities in Haskell a short time ago, and it was a pleasure seeing you again. I hope to attend

the next homecoming festivities and if so, I plan to give another party at the Haskell Country Club. If I can make it, you have an invitation to attend the next party also.

Jan, in addition to the reason mentioned in your letter of why you were born, I can think of another one and a very important one. That is your sparkling personality to bring joy, happiness and pleasant memories not only to your family, but to other friends and acquaintances as well. I feel fortunate that I am one of those and that I can call such a delightful young lady as you my friend.

It sounds like you're making excellent progress in school. Keep it up.

You'll make it. I am sure of that.

Thanks for bringing me up to date on the football team. I'm confident that they'll beat Eastland.

With warm regards.

Sincerely yours,
Charles B. Thornton

Bates' father was an oil well fire fighter during the depression. He married his childhood sweetheart, Sarah Alice Bates, on July 13, 1912. He was 21; she was only 18. With shiny, black hair and sparkling blue eyes, she was considered the prettiest girl in Goree, Texas.

Despite the love that drew Alice and Tex together and which lingered until death, their marriage started to crumble not long after Charles Bates Thornton was born on July 22, 1913. Contemporaries of the young couple said the source of incompatibility lay in a clash of temperaments, he – fiercely independent and she with a dominating personality which expressed itself in a warmhearted, but strict moral code. Tex Thornton wouldn't be domi-nated by anyone -- least of all, his wife and her family. It didn't help matters that the newlyweds, by force of circumstances, resided with her parents.

Since there were limited employment opportunities in Goree, young Tex struck out on his own, seeking wider horizons. Though their marriage ended in divorce, Bates never felt his father deserted him. On the contrary, money and clothes arrived regularly during his childhood, and an early present from his dad was a shiny new bicycle. Plus, there were visits by his father.

Living with his mother, for whom his love and loyalty became profound, so there was an obvious setting that would foster resentment. Not so. Instead, Bates acquired a growing respect for his absentee father -- respect that bordered on awe. Two qualities stood out about his father. Bates loved his aggressive philosophy which embraced change instead of fighting it, plus his dad's equally aggressive pattern of welcoming risks and their accompanying rewards. his equally aggressive philosophy of welcoming risks and its potential reward.

It was reported that his father was commanding fees of up to $10,000 for fighting a bad fire. This prompted some to say he could have done more financially for his son. Not so. It was his nature to be generous, and he seemingly gave away his money as fast as he made it. In fact, hitchhikers Bates' father was befriending murdered him.

Bates got his love for horses from his father. Even as a child, Bates had an uncommonly keen mind. He wanted facts and upon acquiring them, he reasoned logically. Very early, Alice talked to Bates as an equal and confidant, insisting that he accept responsibility in return for her confidence and pride in him, as well as her affection. Young Bates, with a strong yearning for approval, became profoundly and permanently aware of the value of a silver coin and the sweat it represented.

When Bates was in the second grade, they moved from Goree to Haskell. Bates' mother took a sales job at a military store while living at the home of her younger sister who had married a man named McDonald. Here was inflicted his first childhood wound. Living with relatives is greatly different than living in one's own home. Then, his mother married a veterinarian named Dr. A. J. Lewis, at which time he became a step-child. The family eventually included two boys and a girl. Though Dr. Lewis tried hard to treat Bates like one of his own sons, but Bates grew up realizing his life was "different" as a youngster living with a step-father who was married to his mother, a divorced woman.

Wallace Sanders was to become Bates' good friend, blessed with everything Bates had longed for -- mostly security. Further, Wallace -- like Bates -- had guts, charm and pride. Over the years, Mrs. Sanders treated Bates as if he were her own son.

Bates developed strong religious values from his mother and from a remarkable man who was a minister at the Methodist church, Doctor E. Gaston Foote. Bates thought so much of Dr. Foote. (The late Dr. Foote is considered a giant in Methodism. Eventually, he would be viewed as an outstanding author and pulpit giant, serving many years as senior minister of Fort Worth's First United Methodist Church.)

From his Haskell days, Bates became self-reliant, never forgetting, though, how lucky he was to live in America and to have a mother who demonstrated that true wealth lies in how much one does for other people.

Dr. Lewis later moved his family to Lubbock, where Bates enrolled at what was then called Texas Technological College, which had opened its doors only eight years before to 1,000 students. It was the beginning of an enduring bond between Bates and his alma mater, and the bustling city of Lubbock, whose citizens considered their city to be the capitol of greater West Texas.

Bates visited Lubbock's First Methodist Church where Flora Laney, a tall sophomore from Fort Worth, with a rich contralto voice, had been the choir soloist. Whether piety or music or infatuation inspired him, freshman Thornton chose to attend this church regularly. Though he was president of his Sunday School class, he didn't really begin a relationship with the alluring contralto until several years later.

In fact, during the summer of 1933, Bates returned to Haskell in a business venture with his friend, Buford Cox. It didn't work out, however, and slightly more than a year later, Bates visited a young freshman congressman from his district, the late George W. Mahon, at the latter's office in Colorado City. (Mahon, with a half-century or so of public service, himself was a graduate of Hardin-Simmons University.) Bates hoped to get a letter of introduction and advice on how to secure a job with the WPA.

(Works Progress Administration begun during America's Depression years) Congressman Mahon gave him both the letter and the advice.

Bates secured travel money through a loan of $50 from the Haskell Bank. The note was signed by his friend, Tom Davis. Bates packed his best suit of clothes and boarded a bus for Washington, DC. As it rolled eastward, he thought of his mother's parting words. "I know you are going to make something of yourself, which means you won't be living at home anymore. But remember, your home will always be here when you come back." Bates had every intention of doing just that.

In Washington, he took a job with AAA (Agriculture Adjustment Administration) earning $1260 a year. He was promoted to Junior Clerk, which paid $1440 annually. Then, as if on annual cue, he was promoted to Junior Statistical Clerk with an agency called WPA (formerly the Federal Relief Corporation), then to Statistical Clerk with PWA (Public Works Administration), and finally to the U.S. Housing Authority, the latter paying a "whopping" $1800!

In this latest employment, he noticed a fellow worker from Fort Worth, one Elizabeth Gilfillan, to whom he introduced himself. It turned out she already was married, but upon learning Bates had attended Texas Tech, she mentioned, "Perhaps you knew my sister there, Flora Haney. Soon, the conversation turned to Flora's voice, her solos at First Methodist Church, and so forth. "She's visiting Gil and me," Elizabeth said. "You must come over for dinner."

Providence? Blind hog luck? Whatever, Bates found himself in point blank range from Miss Haney, across the dining room table from this West Texas beauty. No regime, plan or military regiment could have prevented his being immediately smitten. Not so, however, with Flora, who, though impressed by his inquisitive mind and progressive outlook, tired soon of statistical subjects. He was all about what years later would become computerization, speaking of machine records, punch cards and new tools for government, industry, business and defense.

Though she found him handsome, she found herself looking at her watch. Far from being swept off her feet, she felt her sister had perhaps built him up a bit too much. But, yes, Flora agreed to see him again. Bates, perhaps sensing "dud qualities" which may have been sensed at dinner, was not about to let her languish from lack of attention, and an "uneven" courtship was begun.

Soon, Bates transferred from George Washington University to Columbia University, where he earned a B.G.S. degree at night school. Many evenings, he'd stretch out on the carpet in Flora's apartment, where she'd drill him on his homework until he knew it better. She'd been in a road show that turned out to be a flop, and she was on the verge of purchasing a one-way bus ticket to Fort Worth when Bates came back on the scene. Truth to tell, she was still smoldering from heated words that had been exchanged during their last meeting. Yet, she painfully missed his company. "Why don't we get married next weekend?" Bates suggested, and they did.

They were married in a hastily-arranged marriage at a Methodist Church in April 10, 1937. It was attended by the Gilfillans and a few close friends, including Charlie Brooks, now Director of Labor Relations for Texaco. Brooks clearly remembers a "young man who knew where he was going." He recalls their getaway from the church, and financial limitations that allowed a three-day honeymoon in nearby Richmond, VA. From the Jefferson Hotel there they could see the beautiful Shenandoah Valley, spring blossoms peaking.

They returned to a one-bedroom apartment on Gerard Street, welcomed into Washington society by George and Helen Mahon, and other notables. Flora recalls earlier conversations about wealth early in their married life. When he shared his dreams, though, topics drifted to the importance of proving oneself and achievements of real value. "Money is part of it," Bates said. "You can't be proud with a hole in your shoe."

With his Business Administration degree from Columbia, Bates qualified for promotion in 1938 to Assistant Statistician at the U.S. Housing Authority, and a salary of $2600. (When he transferred to the War Department in 1941, Bates was earning $4600 per year.) Soon he was a member of the U.S. Air Force. He was promoted to major of the Statistical

Control Staff of the Air Force the same day Flora promoted him to fatherhood. Charles Bates Thornton, Jr., arrived the same day -- May 8, 1942.

At times, Flora felt she was married to a military man who was "MIA." This time, though, the initials stood for "Mission in Action." He saved the government millions of dollars during World War II, but this financial genius was rarely at home. I wish we had him around today to get our country out of debt! Truly, Bates pulled himself up by his bootstraps, literally helping to shorten World War II. He was one of the "Whiz Kids," already thinking about his future when V-J Day came. Flora and Bates had a second son, William Laney, who was born March 26, 1945.

Bates went to work for Ford Motor Company. Though they were back on their feet financially, he was dissatisfied with major company decisions, so he decided to take a job with the Howard Hughes Aircraft Company. He said he could never find Hughes, though, so he bought his own company.

He bought the Litton Company from its founded, Charles Litton. Pulling out all the stops, he flew to NYC, persuading Litton to accept a down payment of $300,000 in cash toward the purchase price of slightly more than one million dollars for Litton's sole ownership of 1,239 shares of common stock and for patents, applications and disclosures. There are many accounts of Bates business acumen. Suffice it to say that Litton soon was a multi-billion dollar company, and that Bates won numerous national honors, including "Man of the Year."

It was said that he never forgot being poor, so when he identified a young man or a young woman who wanted to go to college, he'd pay their way, and he also made substantial gifts to the Methodist Church in Haskell. He helped so many people, and touched so many lives.

At Christmas, he sent me beautiful cards, always accompanied by boxes of candy or cheese. I've learned that he sent similar gifts to numerous other people. We've exchanged many letters. I have, as you'd guess, kept all of his, and I intend to always have them. He also sent me a beautiful diamond fire ring, along with the sweetest letter. When I got it, I was about the happiest girl in town. He gave rings to other people, too, calling them "friendship rings."

After first meeting me, he asked Bob and Anita Herren about me. (Their daughter, Jan Herren Gannaway, is a close friend, and was in my high school graduating class.) They told Bates about my daddy dying at a young age when I was 10 years old, and that I was trying to get my HSU degree. They explained that it was taking a long time, because I could take just six hours at a time. (That's all I could afford, and many times I'd get sick and have to drop out.) He thought my determination was to be admired. Admittedly, I'd made a strong impression on him.

Everyone went to Ruby's house during homecoming. Ruby is sort of kin to Bates in a "roundabout way." He came again to the next homecoming. I was so excited, seeing him once again at the HHS Friday night football game. Once again, he hugged me and my mother. It was raining hard, so we went home early. (Besides that, we were losing the game!)

Later that night, Ruby called, saying Bates wanted to see me over at Ruby's house. Ruby and I have been close friends for years. Mother, Aunt Vanna Lee and I all piled into our car and drove to Ruby's house. Bates and I hugged each other -- like a father and daughter would -- and it was great to see him again in this crowd of about 15 people. I gave him a picture of myself once, and he told me later that he showed it to his friends and bragged about me.

An hour or so later, Bates said he had a gift for me, but it was in his jet plane out at the airport. Mother, Aunt Valla Lee, Bates, Lena Bell (a close friend of Bates) and I drove to the airport. I was permitted to look inside the jet plane, and felt I was in a magical place when I saw its interior, even where the pilot sat! It was the stroke of midnight when he handed me my present -- a new electric typewriter and an envelope containing $110 in cash. I asked Lena Bell if I could sit in the front seat on the way back. I knew if I didn't ask, it would never have happened. On the way home, I told him, "You are just like Santa Clause." Bates laughed, and it was 1 a.m. when we got out of the car.

The next day, we saw him again at the homecoming. We made many pictures that will always be prized possessions. We saw him again at the country club that night, where he so enjoyed visiting friends. I watched him from a distance, thinking about his mentioning he enjoyed walking around the square at 2 in the morning. He was home again.

One time, Bates brought Lena Bell's two daughters back to Haskell with him to surprise her. I knew one of Lena Bell's daughters, Ralna English, was on the Lawrence Welk TV show every week. She is a beautiful girl and has a gorgeous voice. I used to listen to the Lawrence Welk show every week. I love musical shows. I had never met Ralna or her sister in person. They had heard about me from Bates. It was thrill for me to get to meet them both in person. We had our pictures made together; I happily showed them to everyone. Another time, Bates ran into a Haskell High graduate in California, and he brought Roy with him to the next homecoming. Roy graduated in Mother's class, and they had never been able to track him down. He came to every homecoming after that.

He missed the next homecoming, but lit up the next one with his presence! He didn't arrive until Saturday afternoon, I heard his plane approaching and my heart raced with excitement. Bates made homecoming alive! He sat down beside me, and I never heard another word the speaker said! Mother was disgusted with me, because she hard of hearing and asked me what had been said!

Sunday morning after church he called my aunt's house to see if was there. We were staying there during homecoming, because we had already moved to Abilene. Bates talked to my mother, asking if I was there. "I am coming to see her," Bates announced. He brought Ruby every time with him to keep people from talking. He didn't want to harm me in any way; however, it didn't completely stop gossipers. I always just smiled, thinking some people wouldn't believe me if I told them we were never alone. After one homecoming, one woman asked, "What would you do if he brought his wife?" I had a quick, sincere answer: "I wish he would bring her, because I'd love to meet her." This really SHUT HER UP. His wife knew all about me!

Another time, he brought me a beautiful clock, a Cross pen and pencil set and a $100 bill. I was on cloud nine, again. I asked, "What am I going to do with you?" He laughed, "Keep me, I hope!" I assured him we'd all keep him.

Two more years went by, and I learned Bates was coming to homecoming again. Bates, the friend, meant much to me, and I appreciated his gifts, too. Alas, this time when he arrived, the program was almost over.

Prepared to be disappointed, I heard Ruby say, "There's someone who wants to see you at the end of the building." There he was, making videos of everyone present. He motioned for mother, my aunt and me to get in the video with him. I hated to because I sound like Donald Duck on recordings, but I couldn't disappoint him. The others spoke first. When it was my turn, I said a few words about myself. Then he stood by me, saying, "This is my friend, Jan Eastland, and I am very proud she is my friend. We have been friends for nine or ten years now. She is attending HSU and I am very proud of her. She writes me about her progress in school."

I couldn't believe his remarks. That night, we went, again, to the country club to see everyone, including Bates, of course. He showed the videos. He said he wished he'd videoed the proceedings years ago, but didn't think about it until now.

The next day, he gave me a reproduction of *McGuffey's Reader*, a calculator, a leather briefcase, another beautiful diamond fire ring and $250 cash. I wear his rings all the time to remember him by and to tell everyone about how wonderful and generous he was. And how his grand support and encouragement took me to the moon and back.

I learned much later of a talk Bates had with my Uncle Cecil. His account brought tears to our eyes; it was a beautiful story. I think of it often. Bates wanted to know if anything could be done medically for me. "I'd pay for it," he said. Cecil indicated that nothing could be done. "Jan is so pretty and intelligent. Beside my wife and children, I care about no one else more than Jan. I show her picture to everyone." He said he knew I got excited when he brought gifts, but "it means a lot more to me."

That meant so much to me. I cried when Cecil told us. That makes up for everything I have been through. All of my struggling has somehow been worth it. I will always remember him, and I will always treasure his friendship. His paternal love and his interest in me were so powerful that only God could have caused it. He cares about people, and I think it is wonderful. Do you remember when I said I didn't understand why my daddy was taken from me at such an early age? God did not cause it. It just happened. Bates could never take daddy's place in my heart, but God sent Bates to help me in many ways, and to show me He still loves me, and that I need to be reminded of that.

God sent Bates to uplift my spirits. Boy, did He ever! How grateful I am that God did this wonderful thing for me, because He has certainly blessed my life in many ways. I must be special to God. My daddy was a fine man, and Bates was, too. Isn't it ironic they both went Haskell High School never knowing that they'd someday share in my life and influence me to strive higher and higher. Bates loved me like a daughter he never had, with pure paternal love and admiration for me, and I returned that love. I have never been so blessed in my life. So remember this account when someone dies and you don't understand why! God never takes anything away from you He doesn't replace it with something better. He took Daddy away, but he sent Bates to take an interest in me and to take Daddy's place where he left off. Isn't that wonderful?...

The men of Haskell, members of the HSU faculty, the men at the West Texas Rehab Center, men of Calvary Baptist Church and The First Church of the Nazarene and the men at my work have combined to be father figures to me. I know Daddy is smiling down.

The next homecoming was not a happy occasion. We learned that Bates had incurable cancer. I knew I hadn't heard from him in a long time, but I thought he was just busy. Then I figured out that he was trying to spare me from the hurt that he knew I would feel. I wish I could have seen him one more time, and I will when we all get to Heaven. He really suffered. Bates' one fault was that he smoked. The cancer had spread all over his body before it was diagnosed. I wrote him a letter when I found out, and Flora read it to him. I said, "I would give all the money in the world, if Bates could just live." Flora said the letter meant a great deal to him. He was buried in Arlington National Cemetery. There'll be more of his story later in the book.

Mother retired in 1974, and we moved to Abilene. I was still taking classes at HSU. There we were close to many friends, including Sam, a special friend, and the same is true of her sister, Jackie. Helen and Buck were their parents, and Helen used to sew for me. Sam married Bob; they lived other places, but returned to Abilene.

Jackie and Dan lived in Abilene, too, and they had two little boys, Biff and Tray. Sam and Bob had a little girl named Nicki, who became my adopted niece. I just loved my precious memories of those days. After we moved to Abilene, I took Nicki to the movies often when she was a little girl. When Nicki was little girl, I took her riding on the city bus to downtown Abilene. We went into several stores, riding the elevator in one and stopping in an eating place. Simple pleasures.

When Nicki was older, we went to the annual haunted house HSU had each Halloween. Everyone enjoyed it but me. One night, hearing more screaming kids than ever, I entered a room that was totally dark and tripped over a cord strung across the floor. Mother thought I had fainted. I could not make her hear me over the kids screaming, but I finally got her attention. That was the scariest haunted house I have ever been in. I never heard as many screaming kids in all my life. They all thought it was pretty funny; I didn't!

When we moved to Abilene, Mother and I did not know what we were getting into. We had always lived in a small town. Everyone respected everyone else.

We moved into a low rent-housing unit. No telling how many children I have taken interest in or adopted. Children are our future. We are truly interested in them, and can't stand to see children abused or neglected. One boy was saved because of my interest in him. His father didn't care anything about him, and his step-mother locked him outside in the heat of summer and cold of winter, allowing him back in only at bedtime. He had nothing to eat or drink, except from the water hose. His father had a little girl by his second wife, and they treated her much better. I took an interest in him. I bought him some toys and got him started at the YMCA. He had only rocks to give me to show his love and appreciation.

We asked his parents if he could go to church with us one Sunday night. To my surprise, they allowed it. He wanted to sit down close to the front, and during the invitation he said he wanted to respond. I was not sure if he understood what this meant. I asked him to wait until the service was over, and at that time we'd visit with the youth minister. He understood the plan of salvation, and wanted to accept Christ as his Savior. On the way home, Kenneth said the smartest thing a 10-year-old could say. "Now I know what's the matter with my family." Chill bumps went all over my body. I gave him a Bible and I did not want to take him home. Later he lived at the Ben Richey Boys Ranch. Visiting with his dorm parents, I told them there was nothing wrong with Kenneth, just his parents. They said they already knew that!

While I was still going to HSU, something wonderful happened to me. In fact it was the greatest thing that has ever happened to me. It was when my prayer partners came into my life. They have helped me through a lot of physical pain and unnecessary mental pain. I was struggling in my Christian life until a fine Christian lady named Katherine asked me to be her prayer partner. At first I said, "No," and then I said, "Yes!" I do not know where I would be today, if Katherine had not have asked me to be her prayer partner. God has answered so many prayers. Katherine, with God first in her life, was a special person. The devil makes people blind. Katherine and I were prayer partners for about ten years, both growing spiritually during this time.

Katherine was in mother's Sunday school class and was a special friend for years before we became prayer partners. I will love her for the rest of her life. I was physically, spiritually and emotionally sick when she asked me to be her prayer partner. She and God saved me from sheer disaster. She always told me that it was more a blessing to her than it was to me, but I can't imagine this to be true. When you have that kind of relationship with a person, each must truth the other to respect confidences. Katherine was that kind of person. She also had a handicapped grandson; this gave her special insight into understanding the problems of a handicap.

Katherine had been sick in the past, and she promised God if He'd heal her, she would spend the rest of her life in service to Him. She kept her promise. I wish we could number all the times He's answered, but there's no way. We used the Bible scripture that says, "Where two or three are gathered in my name, I will be there also." Katherine never judged me. Katherine, with God's help, kept me going through a difficult period in my life. Having a prayer partner herself could have helped Mother, but she would not do it.

Mother, a very private person, found it hard to share her feelings She never could understand I didn't want her to change herself completely; but I did want her to depend on God more to make things more pleasant between us. That could have made her a happier person, which is all I wanted. She was afraid to get close to God, because Harry went mentally ill over religion; however, this was the devil's tool he held over her head. The whole family was scared of mental illness. Cancer is the same way. People are scared to visit cancer victims, some even afraid they'll "catch it."

When judgment day gets here, a lot of people are going to be surprised about how the devil worked in their lives. God gives us enough ability to see these things, but people ignore it. They are afraid other people will make fun of them if they get close to God. Mother was so stubborn that she was determined not to change herself, and she was so set on it, that it stood in the way of becoming what God wanted her to be. God wanted her to be a happier person, and so did I.

Mother was a great lady in many ways, and I will always love her. She was an inspiration to many people, but think what she could have been had she had turned her life completely over to Him. She would admit this to me. She knew what she was doing to herself, but she wouldn't change. The devil sure did a job on her; I don't mean she wasn't a Christian, but she could have been a powerhouse for God.

Judy was another powerful prayer partner. She lived near me, and we were prayer partners for about two years until she moved away. Judy's husband was an HSU student. Then God sent me another one who was manager of the HSU student union building. Pat was my prayer partner for about 10 years, and became a wonderful friend. Later, she moved back to Maryland to be near her parents. Married earlier, she had a son named Kyle. In Maryland, she married Jay, also a divorcee who had a daughter. Though she had gone to church all her life, Pat had not become a Christian until after her divorce. Jay also became a Christian after his divorce. After they were married, they decided to return to HSU, where Jay would study for the ministry.

Pat and Jay were "pistachio nuts." We had so much fun together, and I ate many meals with them, even if only peanut butter and jelly sand-wiches. Jay and Pat were both funny. Their children were very dear to me and still are to this day. They are Ruthie, Jim Bob, Kyle and Robert Lee. I watched them grow up, and they brought much joy. I never did get to meet Jay's daughter, but I wish I could have. She lived with Jay's mother. Pat helped me through a lot of physical pain, and I will always love her for that. I had severe pain in my neck for nine or ten years, and she and God kept me going. Jay got his degree from HSU, then received his master's degree, as well. In the meantime, he pastored several churches in the area. I went to hear him preach several times. They pastored a Baptist Church in Nolan, Texas. Once a month Mother and I drove up and had dinner with them. We still shared and prayed together. Pat never let me down, and vice versa.

They moved to Fort Worth so he could study at Southwestern Seminary. After Jay and Pat moved to Nolan, we prayed for another prayer partner for me. Soon Dennis, Arleen and Janna Hope moved into our apartment complex, upstairs and across the hall from us. The day I met Arlene, I asked right away if she'd be a prayer partner. Guardedly, she said she'd discuss it with her husband, and thankfully, they agreed!

Arleen has a retarded brother, which make her exceptional in every way. She, too, had an understanding of handicapped people and their problems. I think it is more than coincidence that all of my prayer partners except two have had handicapped people in their families. I think God planned it that way. Arleen had such a special interest in my work with the children at the Rehab, and will never know how I treasure the times we shared together.

Sam and I were prayer partners, too and Sam is a treasure. She helped support me in many She kept me going, along with the help of God, and is a real witness for God. She kept me going along with the help of God. We are still praying for the children at the Rehab. She does not realize how much she added to my life or how much I love her. Sam brings joy to my heart and to my life.

I had another prayer partner named Barbara Cass. Her husband was pastor at our church. I am a member of Calvary Baptist Church in Abilene. It is a very warm church. We were prayer partners only about two or three years, but I grew to love her, and she grew to love me. Barbara said I helped her a lot with my good attitude, and maybe I did. However, she helped me, too.

Another one of my prayer partners was Billie Perry. You are probably wondering how I found my prayer partners. Quite simply, God worked it out. I start praying, God lays an impression on my heart and He works it out. Billie's husband was pastor at our church. Billie had a lot of health problems; we prayed 15 minutes every Wednesday night. However, she was so busy, we didn't get to know each other in a deeper way. Billie had a handicapped little boy in her family, too. She understood the problems of handicapped children and their families.

Charlotte Bridges had been a special friend for a long time. She has been a lot of help to me in many ways, including "prayer partnering." God has answered a lot of our prayers. When she and her husband, Dr. Bridges, went to Hong Kong for six months, I really didn't want them to go. He's there to teach, her to serve in missionary work. So, I needed another prayer partner to fill in for Charlotte.

Doreen Morris' name popped into my mind. She and her husband, Gene are fine people. I have known Doreen for 40 years. Doreen is going to take Charlotte's place, and I told her she's going to get a blessing out of being my prayer partner. Doreen responded that we're "going to be friends from now on." Each prayer partner has a special place in my heart, because I will always be eternally grateful for what they have done for me. They also help me keep going. I pray that I've been blessings to them, too. There are several others who have "'partnered" with me, including Jeri, Lucille, Mitz, Jesse, Floy, June and Jane.

In college, I really enjoyed my classes in psychology. Some of my wonderful teachers were Dr. and Mrs. Ford and Dr. Rod Cannedy. I also took geology under Dr. Harrison. He also was a grand teacher. I took English under Miss Rogers and Miss Rudd. I enjoyed all of my teachers, and they also saw great potential in me. My dorm mothers, Miss Culpepper and Mrs. Hicks, were good to me, too. They took loving care of me. My other teachers are too numerous to mention. I had another sociology teacher named Mr. Dan Cooper. He was a very good teacher. Dr. Greenfield stayed about seven years at HSU, and he, too, was a very good teacher who saw great potential in me. Dr. Beasley meant more to me than he will ever know.

During registration at HSU, for the "umpteenth time," I met Dr. Julian Bridges. He made a wonderful impression on me. Dr. Bridges and his beautiful wife Charlotte were missionaries to Old Mexico for about 25 years before going to HSU.

It was love and admiration at first sight between Dr. Bridges and me. Handsome, with the prettiest curly hair, Dr. Bridges encouraged me in my field of sociology, and saw potential in me. A godly and highly intelligent person, Dr. Bridges and his wife mean more to me than I can say. God had sent me another father figure! Dr. Bridges is a mess and a "walnut." His tests are hard! I made B's in most classes, but I was lucky to get C's in his.

Sometimes I'd get mad during his 4-5 hour tests, which I sometimes had to return to complete. A halo always appeared over his head, however, so how can anyone stay mad at an angel?

I made higher grades in Spanish than I did on Dr. Bridges' tests Dr. Joe Alcorta, my Spanish teacher, is a "Brazil nut." He was a mess! He and I still joke back and forth all the time. One day he asked me a Spanish question, and I didn't know the answer. LDr. Alcorta said, "Do you want

Jan's graduation from Hardin-Simmons University – a very happy day in 1978!

me to throw this book at you?" I answered, "Let it fly," and everyone in class started laughing. I asked him one time, "How come Dr. Bridges loves to have me in his class and you don't?" Dr. Alcorta said, "Dr. Bridges is a hypocrite, and I tell it like it is." I told him to "Shut up!" He laughed, and I now reluctantly admit I enjoyed his class!

After 17 years, I, Jan Camille Eastland, graduated from Hardin-Simmons University. I couldn't believe it when that wonderful day arrived. It was Mother's Day, and I could not have given my mother a better present. We sent out invitations to all of my friends, family and supporters. We requested no gifts. However, they didn't listen to us. I received 190 cards and letters wishing me well on this, "my day." I also received money ($460) and numerous gifts. I had so many "thank you" notes to write, which I was glad to do. Bates sent me $50.

Dr. Jesse Fletcher handed out diplomas. He had been HSU president only two years when I graduated. I love and admire him very much. When I crossed the stage, he said, "Nothing gives me more pleasure than to give you a well-earned degree. You have worked so hard for it." I received a standing ovation; chill bumps went all over my body. When I returned to my seat, the crowd was still standing, yelling and clapping, including Dr. Fletcher and Dr. Bridges.

After graduation, Dr. Bridges wanted pictures made with me and Dr. Fletcher. Dr. Russell Dilday, then president of Southwestern Seminary in Fort Worth, was our commencement speaker. While we posed, Dr. Dilday said our graduation event was the "most exciting he'd ever attended."

After the picture-taking was over, my friends held a reception in my honor in Moody Center, with more than 50 people from Haskell and other parts of Texas attending. My mother was so proud of me. It made me so happy to think I was worth it. My fellow graduates of Haskell High took up a collection without my knowing it, and I was presented a diamond necklace, along with a card the entire class had signed.

A reporter from the *Abilene Reporter-News* interviewed me. Two articles about me appeared in the newspaper. Dr. and Mrs. Bridges gave me an engraved plaque, reading:

> *"To Jan, the most persevering student in Hardin-Simmons University, graduated 1978."*

And I should mention "cash congratulations" totaling $500.

I admit that there was so much excitement, I forgot my diploma. We raced back to HSU, and thankfully, the diploma hadn't moved! I guess this proves I am a "mixed nut!" I'll blame the mistake on fatigue. I was awfully tired that night, but went to sleep a very happy girl....

A letter from my movie star cousin, Mary Kay Place, and a letter from Dr. Robert Schuller and two newspaper articles follow:

FOREVER FERNWOOD

Dear Jan,

Hi! What a great surprise to receive your letter today!

Congratulation on your college graduation! I am so happy and proud for you! Those same qualities of enthusiasm, energy, tenacity, and determination that enabled you to graduate from college will also make you "the Star "Employee" at your new job!

You are going to have a ball! Things are really busy here. I'm finishing my last 4 weeks of Mary Hartman, and then will rehearse with my band for a singing gig -- real tour. Well, I must go rehearse! I was so happy to hear all your wonderful good news!

Love, Mary Kay

❖   ❖   ❖

ROBERT SCHULLER MINISTRIES

January 28, 1973

Jan Eastland

2404 N. Willis, Apt. 141

Abilene, Texas 79603

Dear Jan,

Thank you, my friend, for your prayers and positive commitment to the Hour of Power.

As we proceed in this New Year, let us greet each day with a smile for God is with us, and with the love, joy, and peace of Christ it will be a happy day!

As you put your trust and faith in God, things will go better and better. He will lead, mold, direct, and shape events so that your life will glorify Him in all that you do and say.

Each of us possesses the gift of prayer -- a gift that is price-less. We at the Hour of Power begin each day by joyfully praising Him and lifting our needs before Him. We will pray for you.

Remember...."God at work in you will give you the will and power to achieve His purpose." Philippians 1:6.

Thank you for sharing your news clippings with us. God certainly has blessed you with special talents. May you always use your gift to serve Him.

God loves you and so do I!

Sincerely,
Robert Schuller

◆　◆　◆

GRADUATE SHOWS 'CAN DO SPIRIT'
By GERALDINE SATTERWHITE
Staff Writer

It has taken 17 years, but come Sunday Jan Eastland will have proved again -- that those who said she couldn't do it -- were wrong.

A victim of cerebral palsy -- a result, doctors believe, of a birth injury -- she graduated from Haskell High School in 1961. Taking one or two courses at a time she completed her academic work at Hardin-Simmons University at the end of the fall semester, and Sunday she will be presented her degree in sociology, graduating with her friends.

She went to work full time Jan 6 in the field she loves. She's a teacher's aide at the West Texas Rehabilitation Center.

When a tiny girl, who has cerebral palsy, knows it is time for her one-to-one session with Jan, she begins to crawl toward the door of a small closet-like room. Jan beckons encouragingly; understanding perhaps better than anybody else does in the world the significance of that progress.

"The other day she said 'Bye.'" Jan relates with pride. "She's a precious child." Her students are all precious to Jan, and not one of them will ever be told he can't do anything he chooses to try. "I just don't think you should tell anybody they can't do things." Jan said.

"People have been telling me that all of my life."

There have been, throughout her life, those who said she would never be able to function in a normal classroom, graduate from high school, attend college, drive a car, major in her favorite field, or hold down a full-time job.

But these people who had not reckoned with what Jan calls her stubborn-ness, which her family and close friends know as courage and determination.

She is 31. She never doubted she would graduate.

"I would just like to say I couldn't have done it except for the wonderful people of Haskell, Texas, and the people at Hardin-Simmons University." Jan admits. "They just loved me and were interested in me and encouraged me. And I had some wonderful teachers through grade school, high school, and college."

Haskell friends have been invited to the graduation ceremony in Behrens Chapel Auditorium by informal notes that say, "No gifts please, Just come and be with me if you can. And meet me in Moody Center after graduation."

They are coming.

"We're so proud of her," said Twyla Pace, a high school classmate.

Jan walked on her toes until leg surgery corrected the problem when she was five years old. She wanted to climbs steps like other kids, and she told her Dallas doctor, and when she went back for a check-up after the casts came off, she made him come outside and watch her do just that.

She took speech lessons in Haskell and tap dancing to help her with her coordination. Her mother considered enrolling her in a special class.

"But I didn't want that, and I didn't do it," Jan explains. Sociology was her field, a high school evaluation test revealed, and it became a goal she never lost sight of. Consensus of an evaluation test at the Rehab Center was that she was unrealistic about what she wanted to do, but a determined Jan Eastland knew better.

Her first counselor at HSU, who is no longer at the school, offered her little encouragement.

" Dr. Guy Greenfield was my next counselor and the first one who said I could do it Then Dr. Julian Bridges took his place and he said I could. Dr. Bridges must have told me a million times how proud he is of me."

It was Dr. Bridges who gave Jan the project of working with a black girl, polio victim in a wheelchair, who was having a hard time getting adjusted to school. The two became fast friends and the talented girl transferred after two years to the University of Houston where she studied journalism.

"Her main problem was that she didn't understand how good people at Hardin-Simmons—at any school—are to the handicapped, " Jan explains. "She's coming to my graduation." Sherwyn McNair, journalism teacher under whom Jan took several electives courses, and Dr. Lana Holland, who taught her special education courses are among the other teachers who were most encouraging. Jan has been asked by Dr. Lana Holland to serve as a resource person, and she will be going back from time to time to speak to her classes.

Jan works with the 3 to 5 year old at the Rehab Center, and by 4 p.m. she's getting pretty tired. "Afternoons I work with five-year-olds," she said. "There is nothing much wrong with them and they do into mischief."

A most rewarding part of her job is counseling with parents of CP children.

❖   ❖   ❖

THE ACCOMPLISHERS: THEY DESERVE SPECIAL PRAISES

Jan Eastland, a Hardin-Simmons University coed, who received her degree in sociology Sunday despite also having cerebral palsy. She is a teacher's aide at our West Texas Rehabilitation Center. What an inspiration she is already, and she will continue to be for others as they try to achieve their goals.

(Source: WTRC Newsletter)

Chapter 6

◆　　◆　　◆

HIGH SCHOOL FRIENDS, STILL AN IMPORTANT FACTOR IN MY LIFE

I went to Haskell Grade School, Haskell Junior High School, and Haskell High School with a girl named Barbara Gene Williams. I call her "B.G." for short. She means more to me than she will ever know. We have been friends ever since we were little girls. Her mother and mine were best friends.

She has got the cutest sense of humor, and we laugh a lot when we are together. It is nice to have friends, and when we can laugh with our friends, it makes life so much better. B.G. says, she "doesn't even think about me being handicapped, since it does not matter to her." Now that is a real friend! What a friend she is to me!

Everyone needs that kind of friend. I am so lucky and so blessed with friends. However, that is partially because I work hard to be a good friend myself. Someone once told me I was and am an outstanding friend. That's true—once I am your friend, I am your friend for life.

B.G. and I keep in touch by phone and e-mail. We even start laughing on the phone. B. G. lives in the Fort Worth-Dallas area. I go see her nearly every summer. We have a fantastic time when we get together. Barbara Gene is a "chestnut," because when we get together, she laughs so hard until she hurts in her chest. I do not know what it is about me that attracts people as friends, but it helps if they are nutty like me! I guess it takes one to know one. She is pretty sane, and I am pretty sane, until we get around each other. Then I do not know what happens to either one of us, because we both get hair-brained.. She was awarded Teacher of the Year, so you know she is intelligent. Her former husband is a very serious-minded person, so he does not know what to think of either one of us. I think he thinks that we are both *nuts*, and he just might be right about the matter in question. When we get together, everything is funny. I will always love her for being such a loyal friend. She does a lot for my morale, since we are such good friends. I just know that I love her so much. I think of her as a sister, since I do not have a sister.

One time I went to visit B.G., and she picked me up at the local bus station. The bus station was closed. I had a bag on the bus, and we went around to put it in her car. By the time we go back to get my other luggage, the bus driver was driving off with my luggage. I looked at B.G., and she looked at me. B.G. said I had the funniest look on my face. I thought to myself. "Well, isn't B.G. going to help me?" We are both college graduates, and we stood there like two retarded people and let the bus driver drive off with my luggage. We thought it was hilarious. We laughed all the way to her house. When we got to her home, we called the bus station in Dallas to see if my luggage was there.

The bus people said it wasn't there, but another bus would arrive around 8:30 p.m., and perhaps it would be on that bus. We were free to "wait and see." We went back to the bus station, and my luggage was not on that bus either. We talked to the bus driver. He unlocked the statin door, and there sat my luggage!. Instead of the first bus driver giving me my luggage, he left it in the bus station. So I finally retrieved my luggage. Then we came to the conclusion, that it was not us who were retarded, but perhaps a bus driver as well! We still don't know why he did it.

Another time I visited her, we went to see the Wax Museum. This occurred some four hours after we had spent looking for it. B.G. said she'd find it if she had to "drive all night," and she almost did! We found it at 6 p.m., with closing time just two hours later. Still, it was a wonderful visit, despite being very scary. The wax figures looked so real -- I remember staring at Billy The Kid with my mind thousands of miles away. Suddenly, a little boy came out of nowhere and touched me. I jumped three feet, well into next week!

Moments later, I saw an eye on one of the wax figures move. "Barb, did you see what I saw?" I asked. B.G. said, "I am afraid I did." We started laughing about that. We saw the wax figure of Elvis Presley. That was interesting, because it looked just like him. We saw the wax figure of John F. Kennedy. That really made an impression on me. Then we saw the wax figures of Jesus and His disciples. They were sitting at the Table of the Last Supper. They looked so real. I wanted to touch them or to talk to them. I was glad our evening turned out the way it did, and so was B.G.

Then still another time, we went to see the filming of the television show, *Dallas.* That was a neat experience. B.G. was excited. I was excited, too, but I was not going to let an experience there ruin my day.

We met J.R. Duncan, the man who owns the South Fork Ranch.. He is a very nice man and nothing like J.R. Ewing on the TV show. The South Fork Ranch is beautiful indeed, and we were made to feel welcome. Before the filming, we looked inside the house. We got to see J.R., Miss Ellie, Bobby, Rae, and Susan. While we were waiting for the filming to get started, Bobby went to get us something to drink. I was standing there, minding my own business, when a dog came out of nowhere and relieved himself on my leg. I told B.G. what had happened to me, when she got back with the drinks? I said to her, "How come it is always me that gets it and never you?" Barb laughed and said," I guess that you are just lucky!" I said, "Thanks a lot! " We stood behind ropes while they were filming. We were standing out in the hot sun, because we forgot our umbrellas. Some people were already sitting on the porch of the South Fork Ranch House. We wondered how they managed that. We were burning up, and the people that were already sitting on the porch wanted us to join them. So we did, and we couldn't believe that we were actually sitting there.

Barb said, "We will have something to tell, but will they believe us?" J. R. had on his bathrobe and a cowboy hat. He looked so funny. They were filming around the swimming pool. J. R. signed an autograph for a little boy in a wheelchair. I thought that was sweet. I wanted to see Howard Keel, but we didn't get to. I always thought he was so cute. Then we went to the barn to watch Rae being filmed with Susan and the horses. We had to go through a cow pasture to get there, and I stepped in cow manure. I told Barb again, "How come it is always me, instead of you?" B.G. said, "You are just lucky" and giggled again. Rae is the sweetest man. After the filming was over, he came up on his horse and shook hands with everyone and wished us a happy day. They had to film the same scene four times before they got it right.

We also went to a big mall with an ice skating rink inside the mall. I had never seen anything like that before. We went to a store called Fifth Avenue and looked around. Then we went to Neiman-Marcus. Everything was so expensive. Their dresses were ugly though. I was surprised. The diamonds were beautiful and expensive. I will always treasure the times I had with B.G. They were always fun.

Another high school friend lives in Dallas, too. When I went to see B.G., I went to see Carolyn, too. Carolyn is a "coconut." She used to come and see me and stay at my house, but every time she came, she either got iced in or snowed in. So she quit coming. She is a nurse at Baylor Hospital, and she is very proud of herself. She loves her job. She is still going to school to learn more. She was head nurse and supervisor in the ward for of premature babies. She was my best friend in high school, and I still love her to this very day.

When I graduated from Hardin-Simmons University, she was very proud of me. As a graduation gift, she paid my way on the airplane from Abilene to Dallas. I really enjoyed the little jet I flew on. Carolyn had the whole week planned in advance. We went to see the musical *Brigadoon*. I really enjoyed that. Then we went to a nightclub play called *South Pacific*. The man who played the lead role had a beautiful body and a beautiful voice, too. The music was so pretty, and it was over before I knew it. I didn't want it to be over, because I was having too much fun. We went swimming with Carolyn's sister-in-law and her two girls. We went to a show and to visit Six Flags over Texas. I had a ball. Carolyn will never know how much I appreciated the trip. I also got to see my Great-Aunt Ann and my Great-Uncle Arnold. It had been a long time, since I had seen them, and I really enjoyed that. Carolyn also took me to see where John F. Kennedy was shot. That tragedy was such a shame. Carolyn treated me like a "Queen for a Week." She really made me feel special.

One evening we were eating supper, and I was telling Carolyn about the time I was working in the post office at HSU with a girl who had emotional problems. She did not like me. Bill Snowden said, "If people can't accept themselves, they can't accept a handicapped person." One day, she screamed as loud as she could. I jumped three feet into the air, and the mail I had in my hands went all over the floor. I could not imagine why she was screaming. I looked around, and there was a little kitten in the post office. I will never know how it got in there in the first place. I wondered if someone didn't put it in there for a joke. That sounds just about like a college student. Anyway, I was telling Carolyn about it, and I was screaming myself to illustrate my story. Carolyn said to me, "Jan, if you scream one more time, I am going to slap you." Naturally, I didn't do it one more time because she meant it. We were in the pep squad when we were in high school together, and we screamed then, too, but it didn't seem to bother her. So I don't know when she developed sensitive ears; that was really news to me.

Then I went to see B.G., and I told her what Carolyn had said to me. She and I thought that was the funniest thing we had ever heard of. We laughed and we laughed. We are still laughing about it today. Every time I think of her telling me that, I start to laugh. I have told the story to many of my friends, and they think it is funny, too. Carolyn paid $169.00 to get me down there and then told me that. What a friend!

I have been to see B.G., and she is married again. The poor man doesn't know what he is in for He admitted that to me on the phone. I have not met him yet. They were not married at the time I went down there on the bus. Well, B.G. did it to me again. Every time I go down there, she does something to me. The bus does not stop in Plano anymore. It stops in another town close by. I told her what time I would get down there, and B.G. said, "That she would be there when I got there, but she was not there." The bus stop was in a bad part of town, and I was scared to death. She drove up about fifteen minutes later. When I got in the car, I told her, "I could kill you." She started laughing. She had a good excuse, but that didn't keep me from being scared to death. I asked her, "What I am going to do with you?" We had a good time laughing. We had to stay in a motel, because she had fleas in her house, and I a breaking out from fleabites. I told her, "Your house is a fleabag." She just laughed. I also asked her, "How did you ever graduate from college? You don't seem to have any sense!"

We went shopping, ate out, and went to two shows. We sure had fun, and we laughed a lot together. We went out to eat with Mike and Vicki, and that was fun. Omega and her daughter, Connie, came after me. I sure was glad. I paid for their gas. At least, I didn't have to ride the bus. We stopped on the way home and went through the Wax Museum before we came home. We sure enjoyed that.

Chapter 7

❖   ❖   ❖

MY WEST TEXAS REHABILITATION CENTER DAYS

After HSU graduation, I went to work at the West Texas Rehabilitation Center. (Actually, I didn't actually get my diploma until the upcoming May graduation ceremony.) I was a teacher's aide, teaching three-year-old children. I loved them.

One small child crawled into the closet in order for me to work with her. Her attention span, extremely short, was perhaps the reason this unlikely setting worked. We were not being cruel to her in any way, but somehow, the experience seemed to increase her trust and confidence in us and helped her reduce distractions. She, as well as the other children, made wonderful progress.

Ken was a mystery to me, as well as to others. He simply couldn't be still. It was my job to potty-train him. I rewarded him with cookies when he did what he was supposed to do, and I was told I did better with him than anyone else. While I appreciated the compliment, I joked that I went to college all those years just to potty-train a little child! Laughter prevailed..

I love my teachers, too. They were so sweet to me, helping to bring out my best. Saundra and Carolyn were good teachers. Saundra had also attended HSU, and she was an excellent teacher. I was amazed at how well she controlled the youngsters. Dusty, a fellow aide, was effective, too.

Unfortunately, I suffered from a pinched neck nerve that was most painful, almost unbearable. Perhaps it was the devil's way of hampering the work I was attempting to do for God. I hung in there for ten years out of sheer determination.

When they moved me to work with older children, I had more than my share of work to do. I hated to give up my little children, because they had blessed my life so much. However, the teenagers blessed my life, too.

Some people don't realize that teenagers are as much work as the little children are. However, I had even more fun with them! I loved my muscular dystrophy boys. They were so sweet. It is very hard for me to understand why these youngsters have to suffer the way they do. Three of them were John Ed, Robert and Charlie; Charlie is now dead. I also taught Terry, who suffered from childhood arthritis. He was a mess, but blessed my life in many ways. He, too, is now deceased, now released from a terrible physical plight. He was easy to admire, a fighter to the end. Not only did he have a terrible physical impairment; he also suffered through his mother's committing suicide. Steroids had stunted his growth, but when he was happy, he was a joy to be around. He greatly impacted my life.

Lisa was in car accident caused by a drunk driver, and she will be in a wheelchair for the rest of her life. How sad! She was so pretty, making considerable progress, but despite her good-natured countenance, Christy had a brain tumor and was partially blind. She was such a sweet girl, and she blessed my life in so many ways. I really loved her dearly, as did the other children. I'll never forget her. Some normal people have the worst attitude, and sometimes I just want to slap them and say, "Don't you know how lucky you are?" If you have your health, you have everything.

Donald was thought to be drowned in the lake, but they brought him back to life. Sadly, his mind was a mess. Oddly, it seemed there was nothing the matter with his body. When he arrived at the center, he acted as though he didn't know where he was, and his speech was bad, too. He took off running one day, and I was lucky enough to call him back. He'd stick peanut butter and crackers in his pockets, lose his pencils and such. One day, I caught him flushing the pencils down the toilet!

I worked with him closely, and eventually, his mind seemed normal, and his speech had cleared up, too. The Speech Department worked with him, too. We were amazed at his progress and were very proud of him.

One day, they decided to relocate a tree from in front of our class-room, since they were adding another room to the building. This greatly upset Donald, since he loved trees. I explained they were going to plant it somewhere else, but he remained upset. He lost interest in school, and much progress went down the drain when he left us when his mother remarried. Sadly, she didn't want to fool with him anymore. We visited them in the country, trying to talk the parents into allowing him to return to us. It did not good. They raised poodles, and it was an awful place. When they didn't care for the animals, could they be expected to care for a handicapped child?

We had two cerebral palsy boys, whose problems I could easily appreciate. Their names were Oscar and Scott. Dawn, also a cerebral palsy victim, too, became a special case. She was the only girl in the classroom for a while, and the boys treated her like a queen. Her grandparents, Mr. and Mrs. Baldwin, take care of her. They'll claim their heavenly crowns. Dawn is so smart, and is able to type with one finger. But, she can't talk, and if someone hadn't taken note, she probably would not be educated today.

All handicapped children, including teenagers, need advocates to stand up for them. My mother and daddy did so for me. Dawn does her math in her head, something I'm unable to do. (Math is my worst subject.) Dawn has the cutest sense of humor and her eyes sparkle. She lights up my life and a lot of other people's lives, too. Even though it was my job to feed her, we had fun together. We shared her sense of accomplishment when she graduated at Cooper High School.

A party was held in her honor at the Rehab Center, and we collected money to buy her a machine which helps her communicate more effectively. She communicates with her eyes, too. She has accomplished so much in her life, and she has touched so many lives along the way.

Shelley Smith was a wonderful person. The West Texas Rehabilitation Center would not be here had it not been for him. It was his dream, and he worked hard to get it where it is today. Because of him, WTRC has grown over the years, and now is essentially two rehab facilities.

WTRC depends greatly on its annual telethon held every year to raise money. It is at the center of fund-raising efforts. Rex Allen and Rex Allen

Jr. return every year to super-charge the telethon, as well as numerous other entertainment figures.

There are many other memories from WTRC. Everyone "picked" on me there, too, even the kids. Henry and Dwayne worked there during the time I was undergoing moist heating treatments. There both redefine ornery; in fact, I can't even decide what kind of "nuts" they are. I guess they would be classified as "litchi nuts," because you couldn't get rid of them, either. Everywhere I went in the Rehab, there they were. Once they approached me with a giant hypodermic needle to "give me a shot." I have no idea where they got it, but I knew they weren't going to use me as a target!

I went to high school with twin girls who have always been so good to me. After graduation from college, they said they wanted to take me out to eat. I gave them directions, indicating I now "live behind Mundons." They thought I said, "I was putting out onions." June said to Jane, "What would Jan be doing putting out onions in an apartment?" They definitely are "pistachio nuts."

When I learned at homecoming that Bates had been seriously ill for quite some time, I learned he had not wanted me to know, realizing it would be upsetting to me. He was right, but I so wish I had known. It was such a shock. I knew that I had not heard from him in quite some time, but I thought he was just really busy. I had written him twice, but had not heard a word from him. He had spent his life helping so many people. I prayed for him and his beautiful family every night before I went to sleep. I could not believe Bates was going to die at such a young age. I was so blessed to get to know him. His lawyer, Mr. Price said he really suffered. That was so hard on me, and I'm sure even more so for his family who were at his side for the whole ordeal.

After I found out he was so sick, I wrote him a letter. I felt like I was losing someone very close to me. Flora told me later that the letter meant a lot to him. Anyway Bates' lawyer called mother one day and wanted to talk to me. Mother said I'd be home around 5 p.m. He called back at that time, informing me that Bates wanted to donate 100 shares of Litton stock to the WTRC. I was stunned, and so was Mr. Smith when I informed him of the gift the next day. Later, it was my pleasure to present Bates' letter and the Litton stock to members of the board of the WTRC. The following articles appeared in the Abilene Reporter-News:

Friendship brings gift to Rehab
By Jerry Reed
Staff Writer

A friendship struck up at a Haskell homecoming several years ago enriched the West Texas Rehabilitation Center today by $6,150. That's the value of 100 shares of Litton Industries stock presented to WTRC board chairman Jim Pope on behalf of Litton board chairman Charles Bates Thornton. Jan Eastland, a teacher's aide at the Rehab Center, handed Pope the stock certificates. Miss Eastland, a cerebral palsy victim from Haskell, brought Thornton and the Rehab Center together, said Shelley Smith, executive director "She had befriended Thornton at homecoming in Haskell several years ago, and through her he became interested in the Rehab Center," Smith said, before the board meeting today. Miss Eastland earned her bachelor's degree at Hardin–Simmons University, six credit hours a semester, by working at the post office, Smith said.

As a client of the Rehab Center, she asked, him if she could have a job "if she ever graduated," Smith said, he told her, yes. The board also presented a 60-day budget for the rest of l98l, with expenditures budgeted at $606,630 and income at $1,609,600. Anticipated income includes $650,000 additional revenue from Joint Venture for Crippled Children, $300,000 in general contributors, and $380,000 in trusts and bequests. Anticipated expenditures are anticipated with the first 10 months' average of $303,000.

Also announced at the meeting was a $96,000 challenge grant from the B.B. Owen Trust of Richardson. When matched by $96,000 in additional donations, the resulting $192.000 would go for remodeling and renovating the neurophysiological center for treatment of brain injuries, plus operation of the center. Smith said the trust is guaranteeing $64,000 out of the challenge grant for the remodeling project. In other business, directors elected Mrs. Bill Shirley of Marfa to a three-year term on the board.

Haskell-born industrialist dead at age 68. Haskell native Charles B. "Tex" Thornton a visionary entrepreneur, who used the post-World War II science and technology boom to build tiny Litton Industries into a giant conglomerate, has died at the age of 68. Thornton, Litton's chairman of the board and recipient of the Presidential Medal of Freedom in October, died of cancer about 11:30 p.m. at his Holmby Hills home," said his son, Charles B. Thornton, Jr. His wife of 41 years, Flora, and his son, a Los Angeles resident and a member of the Litton board of directors, were with him when he died, said Litton spokesman Barney Oldfield. Thornton's condition steadily deteriorated since he learned of his cancer in June, with the cancer starting in his lungs and progressing to his bones, said Oldfield. Yet he continued working out of his Litton office in Beverly Hills until September. "I can't stand useless leisure," Thornton once said. Thornton was president of Litton Industries from 1953 to 1961 when he became chairman of the board. In past years, Litton and its directors have been subject to federal investigation into such aspects of the company's sprawling holdings as shipbuilding contracts and importation of computer parts. Litton has become a major defense contractor.

In 1953, Thornton bought what was then a small microwave company with annual sales of $3 million dollars. Within 12 years, his Litton Industries, Inc. became one of the nation's 60-odd firms to report annual sales over a billion dollars.

In the fiscal year ending July 31, 1981, Litton reported sales of $4.94 billion. "Litton wasn't an accident," Thornton once said. "What we wanted to do was build a broad-based company that was strong in every area, not just running strong on one leg and one weak leg."

Thornton was born in Haskell on July 22,1913, the son of Ward A. Thornton, and Alice Bates Thornton. His father, was an oilman, was murdered by a hitchhiker and Thornton was raised by his mother.

When he was 12 years old, his mother encouraged him to buy land with money earned doing odd jobs. He accumulated 40 acres and at age 14 every store in town would accept his personal check. Thornton dropped out of Texas Technological College (now Texas Tech University) in his junior year-1934- and moved to Washington, where he got a job as a $l, l40-a-year clerk in the Department of the Interior. He later got a degree from George Washington University. He entered the Army Air Corps and set up a training program for 1,700 different kinds of specialists. After World War II, with nine military colleagues, he approached the Ford Motor Co, knowing it was losing money, and offered to bring the company under control. His team was hired by Henry Ford, II.

The management he headed became famous as the "Whiz Kids." The team included Robert S. McNamara, later Secretary of Defense under Presidents Kennedy and Johnson, and then president of the World Bank until this year.

Thornton left the Ford Company two years later and took a job with Howard Hughes as vice president and general manager of Hughes Aircraft. He reorganized Hughes Aircraft, building its sales from $1.5 million to $200 million in five years.

Thornton decided to leave Hughes to form his own company. He bought Litton from its engineer-owner, Charles Litton, for $l million. Inside of three years, the company had annual sales of $100 million. Thornton married the former Flora Laney on April 19,1937. They had two sons. Charles, Jr. and Laney of San Francisco.

On October 9, Thornton was awarded the Presidential Medal of Freedom by President Reagan. He was too ill to attend the White House ceremony, so his son, Charles, Jr., accepted the award on his behalf. Only two weeks ago, Thornton gave 100 shares of Litton stock to the West Texas Rehabilitation Center in Abilene.

Jan Eastland, a rehab staff member and former patient Thornton encouraged in her 17-year struggle to obtain her college degree, presented the stock to the rehab board on Thornton's behalf.

-- Abilene Reporter-News, November 1981

Mrs. Joy Dotson was my teacher at the West Texas Rehabilitation Center; later I was her aide. She was a very good teacher, now retired. She cared about the kids and their education. She was sick a lot though, often depending on substitutes to carry on her teaching.

One of my substitutes is a "pecan nut." Betty was very good with the kids, and had much experience with handicapped children. She was my favorite substitute. We were together four or five months when Mrs. Dotson had extended illness, and at other times, too. Betty and I became friends. One day we needed some help to take the teenage kids to the bathroom. They have to be lifted by men. She told me to go to physical therapy for some help. So I went running down there to get some help. I told one of the girls in P. T, that I needed a man. She looked at me like, what would you need with a man? We both laughed at how I phrased the question. I got some help, and we had a good laugh about how I phrased the question.

We had a cerebral palsy student named Van who was an absolute clown. He loved Willie Wonka and The Chocolate Factory. One day, Van asked Betty if she liked chocolate. Betty answered "yes," and the jokes began about whether she'd like chocolate in her hair. That Christmas, it had been joked about so much I gave him a Christmas present of hair they'd collected at the beauty shop!

Betty and I often ate out and shopped together. She sometimes took Mother and me out to eat, but every time she did, mother did all the talking. So Betty did not take Mother along much after that.

From time to time, I've had severe neck pain. It saps you of your strength and your good emotional health. It absolutely drains, and I was in severe pain for about 10 years. I didn't like it a bit. A writer from the *Abilene Reporter-News* wanted to interview a handicapped person to see how they felt about Elizabeth Bouvia's wanting to starve herself to death. So Mr. Shelley Smith suggested that he interview me. I happily complied. Here's the article:

ANSWERING ELIZABETH
Don't give up, says Rehab employee who didn't
Don't judge another man until you've walked a mile
in his moccasins – an old Indian saying.

BY JERRY REED
Staff Writer

Jan Eastland has enough difficulty walking in her own shoes, but she's sympathetic to Elizabeth Bouvia, who cannot walk at all. Ms. Bouvia is the California quadriplegic who has become known lately for her battle to be left alone so she can die by starvation. Life is not worth the pain and humiliation, she says. Ms. Eastland is on the staff of the West Texas Rehabilitation Center. She herself is handicapped in both arms and legs, although she has the use of both.

Both were born with cerebral palsy. "I understand what she is going through. She's more incapacitated than I am. She can't work; and she's in a wheelchair," Ms. Eastland said. "It's a pathetic situation. It makes me sad." But despite her sympathy for the California woman, Ms. Eastland does not want to see her carry out her wish to die. "It's very sad, because life is a God-given thing." Don't give up hope, she advises Ms. Bouvia and others. And she knows about not giving up hope, when things look hopeless to just about everyone else. Jan struggled l7 years against her handicap to obtain her degree from Hardin-Simmons University. "They said, "I would never be able go to college. They said, "I would never work out here," she said, referring to her Rehab Center job. Discouragement of the handicapped is all too common, and it's best not to listen to negative voices, she said. "Some people will listen to them. I know another girl, in a wheelchair, and they didn't help her. All she wanted to do was to go to college and be a writer. "She could do that, because she could type." She was also a fine writer. Ms. Eastland said, but she listened to "them" and gave up her dream.

Ironically, Ms. Bouvia is trying to fend off unwanted encouragement—not discouragement. She does not want people, able-bodied or handicapped, telling her she should not give up her life. Ms. Eastland said, I don't know all of Ms. Bouvia's circumstances, but it's possible the California woman is unaware of all the help that might be available. "Just because she has the difficulty now doesn't mean that it will last." Mine got better. " A drug that became available in 1963 has helped her physical coordination and her speech, she said. " She never does know what is going to come in the future."

If Ms. Bouvia takes her own life, Miss. Eastland said, she might miss out on the next miracle drug that could ease her pain and disability. " If she would just hang in there, something might happen to lessen the pain, just make her better." Ms. Eastland said She is in pain; and I am in pain. But my pain is better than it was." Some people can deal with pain better than others. I am a chicken when comes to pain." She is lucky that I work at the Rehab Center, where I can get regular heat treatments to ease my pain," Ms Eastland said. Like Ms Bouvia, I also suffer from arthritis. she said. Again she emphasized that she doesn't know Ms. Bouvia's circumstances—whether she has close family members, or whether she has a religious faith to sustain her. Either would influence a desire to live over death.

But Miss. Eastland would still tell her to choose life over death. "I mean we've got to keep plugging along. You can't just give up." The following letter is the one Dr. Bridges sent to Miss Bouvia:

January 6, 1984
Ms. Elizabeth Bouvia, Patient
Riverside General Hospital
Riverside, California 92501

Dear Ms. Bouvia,

I felt impressed to send you the enclosed clipping, which appeared very recently in our local newspaper -- a front-page story.

It is my privilege to know Ms. Eastland personally and quite well. I was her faculty advisor and professor and have become a very close friend, almost a substitute father to her. Her dad died when she was very young. As you can tell, she sympathizes with you, as do I.

We want you to know we are praying for you. I Peter 5:7 has become a favorite Scripture verse, because I have discovered in relating to many handicapped people that it means exactly what it says

We love YOU. If there is anything else we may do, please call on us.

Sincerely,
Julian C. Bridges, Ph. D.
Hardin-Simmons University
Department of Sociology and Social Work

I finally gave up and quit my job out of sheer exhaustion. My faith was weak, and the devil knows our weak spots. Also, my mother was going downhill, so I was under a heavy strain. One thing that I never intended to be was the only aide in the classroom. Waiting on eight severely handicapped teenagers was a heavy load. I enjoyed the teenagers though. And it would have been a heavy load for anyone, especially me. My doctor knew about a cure, but he did not tell me about it. After it was too late, I found out about a pain clinic in the Fort Worth-Dallas area from my pastor, Brother Pat. I almost hope the doctor goes through this same horrible experience I went through. I could have kept on teaching. It would have meant so much to me.

Charlotte Bridges has been a special friend of mine for a long time now, because her husband taught me at Hardin-Simmons University. She has been a lot of help to me in many ways. She knew I had about had it with pain. After Brother Pat told us about the pain clinic in the Dallas area, Charlotte started looking into it and found out that they do the same thing here in Abilene. I had the treatment, and it worked. It is called a pain block. I was never so happy in my entire life. God answered our prayers. My doctor knew about it all the time. I still wonder why it had to happen to me at a time in my life, when I was doing the work I had been trained to do, and I wanted so badly to do it. I was very good at working with handicapped children and teenagers. I also have a special gift working with children. The kids loved me, and I loved the kids. I did a lot of questioning God during this time in my life. I still do not understand it, but I guess someday I will. I was angry about it, because I lost everything at once. I quit watching depressing things on T.V. I bought myself a VCR and tapes and started watching funny movies and musicals. They say that you can laugh yourself back to good emotional health. I became more Bible conscious. I started watching Robert Schuller every Sunday morning. He is so positive and he surely does help me. I am his number one fan.

I am also going for counseling, and I believe I am on my way back to good emotional health, but I still have a long way to go. Praying with my prayer partner has helped me, too.

Chapter 8

◆   ◆   ◆

MY TRIP TO HAWAII

Mother and I were lucky enough to get to go to Hawaii with a tour group from my hometown of Haskell, Texas. My cousin, Paul and his wonderful wife, Barbara paid for the trip. My Great-Uncle Arnold and my Great-Aunt Ann helped Mother and me financially also. Wasn't that wonderful! Paul and Barbara have been a lot of help to me in many ways. They were sweet, sweet people. Here again, God has sent me another father- figure. I am a very lucky person

Nancy was our tour guide. Nancy is a go-getter. We have been friends a very long time. We used to live across the street from her parents and her family and her. I watched her two boys grow up. Her parents were very sweet people. I knew Nancy better than I did her husband. However, he went with us on the trip, and I got to know him better. Since I had never been around before, I didn't know he is a nut. Bailey is a beechnut. Nancy is sophisticated, and she is married to a nut. He would embarrass her, because she was afraid that people would not know how to take him. He says anything that comes into his mind.

We rode the bus from Haskell to Dallas and caught the plane out of Dallas. Then we flew to Hawaii. Mother was in bad shape when we went. She had fallen and broken her collarbone; however, she went anyway. She went in a wheelchair, since she couldn't walk very far. Nancy and Bailey took their son, Sam, just to help us. Wasn't that sweet of them to do for us!

Sam is just like his daddy. He is a beechnut, also. I asked Bailey to come up to our room one day in one of the hotels to fix our TV. He fixed it, and while Bailey was there, I asked him, "Would you please open a bottle of Seven-Up for me?" He did that for me, and then Bailey asked me, "Did you know this is a chaser? What is a good Baptist like you doing drinking a chaser?" Then Bailey said he was going to tell the Baptist preacher what he had seen me doing, when he got back home. I told him "Go ahead and tell the preacher, because I do not care." Well, that broke the ice between us, and Bailey teased me from then on, and so did his son, Sam. We sure had fun fussing back and forth. We really love Nancy and Bailey. They sure were good to us, and we sure did appreciate it.

We stayed in Hawaii eight days and eight nights. The country scenery was beautiful. I have never seen anything like it. I did not want to come home. I hope heaven is that beautiful. I told Nancy this is what I call the Garden of Eden. I bought a beautiful painting of a Hawaiian princess, who died of a broken heart, because she lost her first lover. He had died at a young age, but I don't know why he died. I framed it when I got back home. It sure was pretty, and I am very proud of it.

We were on three different islands, and they were all beautiful. Each island had different scenery. We went to a nightclub and saw a show, and I surely enjoyed that. We had our pictures made with everyone in the group. We were very proud of the pictures. Pictures are such treasures anyway. I will keep them forever.

There were about forty or fifty people that went with us. Most of them were from Haskell, but a few people were not. Nancy and I went shopping one day, and I bought mother and me some dresses. I still enjoy wearing mine. We stayed at a beautiful motel on top of a volcano on one of the islands. I had never seen a volcano before. I thought that was very interesting. We had room service twice, and that was very special to us, because we had never done anything like that before. The food was sure good. We could look out our window and could see the beautiful ocean. That was surely pretty.

They had little iceboxes in every room filled with juices, Cokes, Seven-Ups, and snacks, but if you ate anything you had to pay for it. It was expensive, too. I had never seen anything like that before. We missed out on a lot, because mother was in such bad shape, but I still had a ball. Nancy didn't forget us either. I sure did appreciate that.

Some of the people in our group stayed on a ranch. It was supposed to be the world's largest ranch. I bought a beautiful necklace that I will treasure always, and, of course, I bought some beautiful picture postcards. Everyone treated us so nicely. They treated us like kings and queens, and it made us feel so special. I had always wanted to go to Hawaii, but I never thought that I would actually get to go. Paul, Barbara, and Aunt Ann will never know how much we enjoyed ourselves. We appreciated it, also. Some of the people in our group shared their beautiful pictures with us, and I will always treasure them. I put them into an album, and I get them out every once in a while just look at them. Wasn't that nice of them! I would love to live there.

While Mother and I were in Hawaii, I saw a girl using sign language. She was talking to her mother. She looked at me, and I saw in her eyes that she knew that we were both handicapped. She held the door open for us, so I could get mother into this eating-place. I thought that was neat! The gesture really touched me.

The last place we stayed, we were out on the beach. I tried to walk out to see the water, but I couldn't even stand up on the sand, much less walk on it, it was so thick. I don't see how people do it. So I just stood and watched the beautiful ships go by. They were so colorful and beautiful. I had never seen anything like that either except in pictures. The hotel had entertainment, and we enjoyed that. Some people were dancing, and Bailey tried to get me to dance with him, but I wouldn't do it.

Then everyone went to a luau and had roasted pig. That sure was fun and another new experience. I really enjoyed the food and entertainment. Nancy and Bailey even danced a Hawaiian dance. I sure did laugh at him. He is the biggest nut. We had our picture made with a gorgeous Hawaiian lady. It was a very good picture, and I was proud of it.

On the bus tour we saw a beautiful rainbow in the most gorgeous scenery. I will never forget that scene as long as I live. They made a picture of it. It was so pretty. They had the most gorgeous flowers and trees. The trees had the most beautiful orange blossoms on them. I had never seen anything like that before. We also went through a pineapple plant, where they prepared them to be sold. We saw a sugarcane field and a pineapple field. We stopped at a candy factory, which was very interesting. We saw a gorgeous waterfall in the most magnificent setting you ever saw.

Mother got to do something she had always wanted to do. She got to see Pearl Harbor. Sam went with her to push her in the wheelchair, and he nearly pushed her into the ocean just for pure orneriness sake. He is a mess!

Bailey pushed mother across the street in her wheelchair one night. Mother said, "That was the roughest ride she had ever had." I told Nancy what she had said, and Nancy said, "Oh, I know! He is so rough." Of course, he didn't mean to be that rough. The Street was rough. I made another friend out of Bailey and his son, Sam. I am sure proud of that. I will never know how Nancy saw to it that everyone had fun, and at the same time tended to us and never left us out. She has more energy than I do.

Everyone got along so well on the plane coming back to Texas. The trip back took 25 hours. We got to see the Golden Gate Bridge. I enjoyed that. Mother and I couldn't sleep, so we watched a movie. It was so long to have to fly that many hours. I never saw such a big plane. We were just about to fly into the Dallas airport when Bailey hollered just as loud as he could, "Hey Jan. We just spent the night together." I said, "Bailey, would you please Shut Up!" I turned red in the face. Of course, everyone on the tour knew what he meant, but the other people on the plane didn't know what Bailey meant. They probably thought Bailey and I had really spent the night together. I could have killed him. I told you -- he is a nut. Nancy didn't hear him, thank goodness! When we got off the plane in Dallas,

Bailey said, "Boy, we sure did have fun!" I guess he did, since he had so much fun teasing me. I hate to admit it, but I did, too

I will always love Nancy and Bailey. I will never forget that trip, and the fun we had together. It will be one of my fondest memories. Everyone got along so well. I was amazed at that. We love Nancy, Bailey, and Sam very much. We appreciated what they did for us. I told you there is nobody better than Haskell people, and that proves it.

Chapter 9

◆　◆　◆

THE LORD SENDS A BUNCH OF MARYS IN MY LIFE AND GAVE ME BACK MY SENSE OF HUMOR

We ate out with "Mr. Ornery" -- a true "peanut" if you're keeping score—and he was accompanied by his sweet wife, Jo. As we awaited placement of our order, "Mr. Ornery" -- aka Burneal Watts -- stared at the wall, honing in on the picture of a woman he claimed was wanted by the law. Whoever provided assistance to her apprehension would receive a $100 reward. He pointed at me, telling the waitress, "There she is! I want my money."

This has been -- in a "nutshell" -- the story of my life. I stuck my tongue out at him, and the room rocked with laughter, led, of course, by "Mr. Ornery," and the lady who dropped her pad and pretty much gave up on writing down our orders—they wouldn't have made sense to the cook, anyway! Years ago, the Coasters helped make comic strip figure <u>Peanuts</u> a household word with their song, "Why Is Everybody Always Pickin' On Me?"

Mr. Burneal goes to my church, and is on a long list of friends and loved ones who get many "kicks" in teasing me. On a serious note, he and his wife are very sweet, and, they -- like others -- know I have a streak of "orneriness" in me that's probably several coats thick and makes people feel free to pick on me! Yep, on both my best days and my worse, I'm ornery, too!

Recalled is a story of Mother attending a funeral. She was on a down-hill slide health-wise, and shouldn't even have been driving. However, she dug in her heels, refusing to listen to sound advice, no matter how well intended. Aunt Dodie and I went with her. Right outside of Abilene, we were stopped by a policeman who said she was driving 80 MPH. She felt the matter was open to debate, saying his was "the biggest lie she'd ever heard."(Truth be told, I doubt if she was going that fast. In her later years, she—like most old people—caused more accidents by driving slow rather than fast.) I'm guessing she may have been going 60 MPH as she passed a truck.

We appeared before the Justice of the Peace. I asked him if she looked like a woman who would be driving 80 MPH. No one said a word, and Mother paid the fine. This was at least the second time in her life something like this happened to her. Somehow the world has lots of people who like to pick on little old ladies. Oh, well . . .

Anyway, the Lord sent a bunch of Marys into my life to help me get back to my old self. They are all "crazy"-- and if you've read this far, you realize I typically use the word in a jovial manner. That doesn't mean I don't love them, and, in fact, refer to them as sweet -- a tag I'll give "Mary" who is my counselor at First Baptist Church. She is a special person, and I love her dearly. She is, in fact, the person who suggested I write this book.

Another "Mary" is likewise amazing. She's made of strong stuff; her husband Glen is in bad health due to a heart condition. In addition, he has limited eyesight. She helps take care of him. He is unable to drive, so Mary is the family driver, too.

He, too, is a character, perhaps a "walnut," since he has a very hard head. As to driving, Mary has certainly helped me out, too, since Mother can't drive anymore. Unbelievably, she has a garden during the spring and summer, and she, also, is behind the mower that keeps their lawn in trim. She, also, handles cooking, and most household chores. She is my mother's age (and also went to school with my mother). It's amazing she is able to handle so many duties without forfeiting her good health.

She cans, makes candy, pies and cakes and is commonly a blue ribbon winner at Abilene's annual West Texas Fair. She, also, sews, knits, does other finger work, and her tablecloths are beautiful. She and Glen have three lovely daughters, as well as several grandchildren and great-grandchildren.

Marilyn comes to the 1929 class reunions, so I know her better than I do some of the other girls. She and her husband have arts and craft talents, turning out beautiful work. I have bought some of their things. Marilyn's sister, Glenda, is also into arts and crafts now. This family means a great deal to me.

Another friend -- I'll call her Lulu -- is a "macadamia nut." Lulu isn't really her name, but I call her that because of Lulu on the TV show "Hee Haw." My Lulu is even funnier, a real "Lulu!" I could describe some side-splitting situations, but have thought better of providing too much detail. Perhaps I can pique your interest by mentioning the vignettes include her getting stuck in a square bathtub and a situation at a Catholic wedding where she was unsure if her undergarments were going to stay in place, what with so much sitting, standing and kneeling. Contact me if you want some blanks filled in!

I was in a huff later upon learning that as a non-Catholic, I wasn't required to go through all the rituals folks of that faith do. Oh, there were dozens of other anxious moments at the wedding, but in order to keep this book shorter than *War and Peace*, I'll have to recreate them later by some other means!

Okay, just ONE MORE quick story. One day, Lulu told me she'd never go to a certain grocery store again, "because their grocery carts follow you out of the store." It turns out that some time earlier, her purse strap caught on a cart, so without knowing it, she was pulling eight carts out of the store behind her!

Lulu, in earlier life, had worked the night shift as a telephone operator. One night while drinking a Coke, she spilled it all over the switchboard. A friend recommended that she carefully clean the entire switchboard, from top to bottom It required several hours, but when she finished, it was spotless. The next day when Mitch, her boss, arrived at work, he was puzzled. "Why is the switchboard so clean?" he asked. So, she told him what happened, proving once more, I suppose, that your sins will find you out!

At a family reunion, Lulu and her family were sitting around visiting. They looked up and there was a mouse dancing to some music they were playing. She had never seen anything like that before. I asked, "Lulu, are you sure you're not making this up?" Lulu said, "No! It is the truth." I said, "That is hard to believe!" However, I know Lulu would not lie about it.

One time Lulu went to a funeral back during hat-wearing days. With her hat on, Lulu's ears flopped down. Her friends' hats didn't look any better. At the funeral they sat behind a tall skinny lady whose hat made her look like a pinwheel. They had to hold in laughter, which, I guess, would have cast a pall on the whole occasion! I admit I can pick some of the craziest "nuts" for friends, but I surely do love them! I've noticed that the list of people who used to be happy to go to funerals with me is getting shorter every year…

One time Lulu held a birthday party for me in her beautiful home. I mean she went "all out," providing lunch, a nice cake and dozens of balloons. My friends came to the occasion fully costumed, and Lulu dressed as a clown, complete with a bulbous, bright red nose. She was "topped off" with a red wig Let me simply reiterate, my friends are "off the charts" with tradition, and most of the are determined to be "who they are." They may not be funnier than a barrel of monkeys, but they're funnier than a half-barrel of 'em for sure!

My mother lost her hearing in one ear about 65 years ago. Her "nerve deafness" in that ear was irreversible. They didn't have effective hearing aids for such conditions back then. Therefore, it was frustrating for both of us. other had a hard time hearing me, and with my slight speaking problem, I didn't help matters much!

However, the situation caused several laughable moments, some that didn't seem to be funny at the time. Once, a repairman came to our apartment to fix an appliance. When Earl finished, we paid him and he was on his way. A few days later, I asked, "Mother, do you remember the other day when Earl was here?" Unfortunately, she thought I said, "Let's open another can of beer." I got the garbed message straightened out as soon as I could.

Later, she got a hearing aid for nerve deafness, but by that time it was too late. Besides that, by this time Mother's mental capabilities were failing, so maybe whether she could hear me didn't matter all that much. I was able to get a refund on the hearing aid, but later, when Mom's thinking began to clear up, I wished I'd kept it. Such is life . . .

Chapter 10

❖ ❖ ❖

SAD AND FUNNY THINGS THAT HAPPENED TO ME DURING MY MOTHER'S REST HOME YEARS

Mother had been going downhill for a long time. I couldn't get her interested in anything outside the home. One thing for sure, one can't just sit; going downhill then is inevitable. She was losing her sense of humor, which, to that point, was the major reason we both kept going. I took care of her as long as I could.

Aunt Vera and I realized she had to start walking, but stubbornness prevailed. When she asked where Mother got her stubbornness, I defended myself, saying, "She didn't get it from me, because she was here before I was."

Mother was sleepy all the time. One morning she fell asleep drinking coffee, and the liquid ran down the front of her robe. Such wasn't unusual. Her doctor sensed her seeming resignation from life, and he, too, took note of her fading sense of humor as well as her growing depression. It was later determined that she had water on the brain, an unusual condition among older people. It was determined she needed brain surgery, including shunt implanted to reduce pressure and provide drainage. She made it through surgery just fine. We thank God for Dr. O'Loughlin.

One of my relatives had a stroke about 30 years ago and once again, Dr. O'Loughlin came through. Even though other physicians wanted to "pull the plug," Dr. O'Loughlin wouldn't consent to it. He was her surgeon, and her successful surgery netted her almost 20 additional years of life.

Knowing his success with stoke victims, my mother was confident about his surgery on her. In the time leading up to it, we noticed her considerable odd behavior. One morning, she insisted on toast and butter for breakfast, despite typically eating cereal in the mornings. She insisted that I have toast and butter, too. Later she was two hours late preparing lunch. In a random comment, she asked, "Why would anyone put nuts in a fruitcake?" Once I asked her to get me a Dr. Pepper, but she was at the refrigerator "looking for the TV Guide." The doctor said this was not unusual behavior for stroke victims.

Actually, there were numerous other incidents, including two household fires. Luckily, I was able to put them out, but one caused considerable smoke damage.

Soon, it was evident that she was in no condition to drive. I took possession of her car keys, and it angered her greatly. Likewise, I took over the mail, since she was failing to pay some of our bills. Well, that was another entry on her "mad" list. Since she wouldn't listen to me at all, I called Dr. Kemp, to arrange for her to move to Rice Springs Rest Home in Haskell. (Dr. Kemp is a partner in the rest home. And, before it was called "Hamlin," our town was named Rice Springs.)

They take such good of their patients. Mother had told me years ago that she would prefer this rest home. It broke my heart, but when the time came and she was hard to handle, the decision for her to go to Rice Springs Rest Home was made. She had care needs I could no longer provide. With help from my cousin Bill Eastland in Pecos and Mike Eastland in Arlington, we made the move.

Ordinarily, I would have told Mother what was happening, but her mind was in such shape, she couldn't have handled the news. There's a good chance she would have run away and we might never have found her. When we packed her bags and started to leave the house, she shocked me by saying, "I think Jan is being pretty brave about this situation." For that brief, but important moment, she was in her right mind. Of course, she was angry with me later, and we had to give her a pill to calm her down. I'm not sure she eer truly realized where she was going, and perhaps never did grasp this would be her last stop in this life.

We got to see Mother about twice a month. It seemed she could identify most of the residents, and it was evident she was eating normally again. She'd pretty much quit eating before she left home. This was most surprising -- her failure to eat -- since she'd been really good at it until her final years. Dr. Cadenhead ran tests that revealed she had low blood sugar. With medication she was doing better. She gained back a lot of lost weight, her appetite was back, and her memory cleared up considerably. Her diet was modified, of course. She had loved candy her entire life, but it became a "no-no." The closest she got to it came in the form of sugar free cookies. She, also, enjoyed hamburgers we took for her dinner meal from time to time.

Nurses and the other residents loved Mother, who one day said, "I wish I hadn't quit working." I had a clever response, "Well, Mother, that's why you're here. I tried to get you to work, but you refused, so we put you in the rest home." It pretty much cracked everyone up.

During her early months there, Mother called me on the phone regularly, always asking why she couldn't come home. How she remembered the phone number, I'll never know. She, also, couldn't understand why she couldn't be taken to church. As might be expected, she had many questions for which the answers to her meant nothing. I will always be indebted to administrators of the rest home, Ruth Ann, Jo Ann and Lou Ann. They are the best! I'll always appreciate what they did for my mother to ease many pressures which were stacking upon me during that period of my life. Few people thought Mother would last as long as she did, but she was feeling better at the rest home during her some 30 months there. Her life being extended this long said much about the excellent car she received there.

On one birthday, Aunts Dodie and Vera, Uncle Luther and Kent and Norma came from San Angelo to help her celebrate. Kent and Norman are my cousins. Mother was so happy, she cried when we saw us, but was so excited, she couldn't eat. And, she announced an elaborate plan to get all of them back to Haskell, where they'd all be one "big happy family." She had it all figured out. Her sister, Vera, who had worked for years in the school lunchroom, would cook for a living. Kent, Vera's son, would buy some land to work "near the railroad track," since he loves trains.

I thank God for kinfolks and friends. For example, a cousin, Paul Williams, a man I'd seen only twice in my life, attended Aunt Effie's funeral in Monahans. He was kind enough to take all of us out for steak dinners following the funeral. As we started to leave, he handed an envelope to Rebecca Sue, who, upon opening it, was excited for Mother and me. In it was a check for $900, and this amount started coming from him and Barbara every Christmas. I knew he intended for the money to be used for both Mother and me, and I also knew he and Barbara would be upset if they knew we lived in government housing. Perhaps they thought this might make it possible for us to move to a more upscale place, but Mother had no interest in that. I also knew if I told them where we lived, Mother wouldn't be happy with that. So, I bought things I thought could be converted to cash later, but things didn't work out the way I had planned.

When it was time to put Mother in the nursing home, I didn't have the money to cover the bill. It wasn't a problem I could do much about, because Mother had become totally irresponsible, spending money right and left. As an example, she had, almost literally, 200 pairs of shoes! Though her mind was nearly gone, her ability to spend money wasn't misplaced!

I have decided, though, that God provides the means when we most need it. I started getting checks from everywhere, and my drug store in Haskell and administrators at the rest home were helpful and understanding. What a grand hometown!

When I went to visit Paul at Bill and Billie Nell's home in Pecos, he and his wife said they wanted to help from then on. I mean to tell you Paul and Barbara are saints! Vera helped with Mother's funeral expenses. I am a lucky girl!

While my mother was in the rest home; I was lucky enough to visit Tennessee with a tour group from my church. It was in the fall, and the trees were bursting with beautiful fall colors. I had never seen anything so pretty. The trees were all colors, including red, orange, green, and even purple.

We drove through Arkansas to get there. Arkansas was pretty, too. I had always wanted to go to Tennessee, but never dreamed I'd get to actually do so. We visited the beautiful cities of Nashville and Memphis. I had a ball. Always a fan of Elvis Presley and admirer of his wonderful voice, I never dreamed of getting to see his beautiful home.

Still, I must admit it was rather strangely appointed. There were mirrors everywhere, and parked right there was his pink Cadillac. There were his stacks of gold records, and we saw where he was buried. I guess he's the reason I've always loved country music, and the visit to Tennessee confirmed it. We saw other homes of country music stars, including Dolly Parton's. I have always loved Dolly; she is so happy and full of life

At the storied Ryman Auditorium in Nashville, we were privileged to sing on stage! What a neat experience. We also shopped in some of the country/western star's shops.

Something funny happened at one stop on our trip. Our guide told us to be back at the bus by a certain time. When we got off, everyone went different directions, and no one asked me to go along with them. It was nothing intentional; it just happened. I didn't have a watch to keep up with the time, but I was just about to return to the bus when one of the church members rounded a corner looking for me. Turns out I was late, and the whole bunch was worried about me.

When we got back to the bus, Mr. Ornery, a "peanut," told me, "If you ever do that again, I am going to tie you to the back of the bus and drag you all the way back to Texas." I told him, of course, to "Shut up!" He picked on me during the entire trip, even though he was the bus driver!

Another Nashville stop was at the Grand Old Opry, where, again, we were privileged to sing on stage. We also were privileged to spend at day at an amusement park called Opryland which is similar to Six Flags Over

Texas. Tagging along with the Mims family, I talked Tonya into riding the big roller coaster with me. Upon being strapped in, we were afraid we'd made a big mistake! And we had. Riding it was a thrill, but we didn't ride it a second time! I bought a beautiful skirt at the park; we didn't want to go home!

A friend named Wanda provided much assistance when my mother was in the rest home. John, her husband, has his share of orneriness, and I'll call him a "peanut." We fuss. When I accompany them to the grocery store he argues with me about what I am planning to buy. During one of these sessions, Wanda said, "I am going to leave you two behind. You sound like two old women arguing over what to buy!" I didn't let him buffalo me, though. I bought what I wanted to buy, NOT what he suggested!

Seriously, they are good to me, and I take them out to eat occasionally to reciprocate. I should ad that at one time, she even cooked meals for me, and this was truly appreciated.

When Wanda's girls were little, they were in Mother's Sunday School class. Mother said during Sunday school, the little girls loved to hike up their dresses to show everyone their new panties! There were, of course, many other stories of her class of little toddlers.

Mother often had remarks to say about her surroundings, and as often as not, they, too, produced laughter. Once, when Hazel, Rebecca and I took her to the hospital in Abilene, she picked up a Bible in the lobby. "Look here," she said, "You'd think the hospital could afford to buy its own Bibles." (The Bibles, of course, were placed there as requested by the Gideon's!)

Frank and Mary Anna, the "kola nuts," provided much summer fun during visits to their home during "growing up" years. After Mother went to the rest home, Mary Anna and a friend came to see me, then took me for a visit in Lubbock. (It was during that visit that Mother embarrassed me by calling her visitors "kooks!") I'm sure I embarrassed Mother many times in the past, but during her final years, she got even! Sam, a longtime friend who visited her, probably had the right idea: "Just let her talk," he said.

When Mother went to the rest home, we sold her car to a friend who wanted the vehicle for her daughter, who is clearly a "walnut." She and her husband Bob paid me well for my mother's car. The money was needed, of course, to pay Mother's debts. They also helped in this effort, providing me with the proceeds of a garage sale -- one that netted $500, the most of any such sale I'd ever participated in.

My mother was the worst of pack rats. And she was as stubborn as a mule, always proclaiming, "I yam what I yam," like Popeye would say it.

All of my life, we had big piles of newspapers all over the house. I preferred having a neat house, and neatness was the last thing on my mother's mind. We had lots of fights about this one issue, but they never did any good. Despite my opposition, she kept everything, refusing to even throw away a paper plate. God says in His word that when something is causing a problem, throw it out. If she ever read this passage, it never moved her to apply it in her own life!

Mother and Daddy moved every time we turned around. And even after Daddy died, we still moved a lot. Aunt Dodie helped my mother and me move every time we moved. One time, she said, "My mama and papa were married 50 years, and they didn't have as much junk as your mother." Daddy always said, Elsye could "fill a 10-room house with her junk."

Indeed, Mother had 17 boxes of newspapers piled up against our bedroom window. We couldn't have gotten out in case of fire. The inspector threw a fit, and I don't blame her. I started trying to sneak newspapers out of the house during Mother's naps, but somehow, she always missed them and threw a fit! The boxes of newspapers and hundreds of magazines all went to the dump, but not until Mother had moved to the rest home.

After Mother moved, I needed to I needed to have a car of some kind. I've always been able to drive, and have a license to do so, but Mother never allowed it. I thought about buying a motorcycle, and Wanda said she couldn't quite envision my riding on one! Dolores said if I did, she buy me a red scarf and helmet so I could "fit in" with Snoopy and the Red

Baron in the funny papers. I told everyone and they started teasing me about it.

Landlords Bob and Betty are "filbert nuts" who have been very good to me. Bob started teasing me about it, too. They tell me funny stories about their work. Betty could write a book about being a landlady.

One time, I started getting multiple telephone calls each day. Each asked if I had a box spring and mattress for sale. I answered "no" every time I was asked this question. During another time, repeated calls came with inquiries about a chair and couch. And yet another time, inquiries came about a motorcycle. Still another, calls came for a washing machine. I learned later that these ads, indeed, appeared in the *Abilene Reporter-News*, and somehow, my phone number was in the ads by mistake!

Oh, my wacky friends! Landlord Bob once took my aunt and me to see my mother in Haskell. On the way there, he honked his horn, and I saw no one for him to be honking at. "I'm honking to get the red ants out of the way," he laughed. See what I've had to put up with!

I am going to show you what a grand sense of humor my mother had. Going to school one day, I wasn't looking too well. Mother asked, "Are you going to go to school looking like that?" Saying that I was, she said, "Well tell everyone your name is 'Westland;' I don't want anyone to think you are an 'Eastland'."…We both got a good laugh out of that one.

One day Landlord Bob took our maintenance man, Vick, and me to the courthouse to get our car licenses renewed. While we were waiting on Vick, Bob teased me, saying that he'd heard I'd been attending a Jehovah's Witness Convention being held in Abilene. I told him to "Shut up!" That night, Mr. Ornery called to say that he was going to tell our preacher that he'd heard I was at the convention, and besides that, had been running around with two married men! Again, my quick answer that usually works: "Shut up!"

Some very funny things have happened to me down through the years regarding my being a cerebral palsy victim. However, just about the funniest thing that has ever happened to me occurred many years ago. Keep in mind that some people think all handicapped people are retarded. I was in Eckerd's Drug, and was at the counter to check out. A clerk named Sue asked, "Do you have an attendant?" My mind raced. Why would I need an attendant? It turns out my hearing failed me. She was asking, "Do you have a driver's license?"

Once I was ordering new checks. I asked them if they could add "retarded" to the name on my account. They got tickled, but accommodated me. Ever since then, I've used it as my password. Bank personnel now always expect me to say my code name is "retarded."

My dentist is Dr. Johnny Estes, an "acorn nut." Dr. Kemp recommended him, so why shouldn't I have been expected to go to another "nut." He's a good dentist, though, and I guess it does "take one to know one." He and I kid each other just like Dr. Kemp and I did. During one visit, he told me I'd need a crown. I asked "how much?," and he told me it would be about $300. "I think I'll just kill myself," I joked. His response: "Please don't until after you pay me off!" He laughed, adding, "We may not get your teeth fixed, but we surely do have fun!" On another occasion, he was preparing to do a root canal on me. He asked me not to say a word, then asked his assistant, "Get out that instruction book, and tell me how to do a root canal." I knew, of course, that he was teasing. When he was finished, though, I said, "I'd very much like to get you in my dental chair and do to you what you did to me!". And we left it at that....

Jan's cousin, Mike Eastland, and family

Chapter 11

◆ ◆ ◆

SECOND PHASE OF MY WTRC DAYS
AND DEATH OF MR. SHELLEY SMITH

After Mother went to the rest home, and after I finished getting rid of all of her newspapers, I returned to part-time work at West Texas Rehab. Mr. Shelley Smith invited me to come back, and it gave me something constructive to do. I was open to God's will concerning what I should do in the future.

I worked with a wonderful woman named Jerry, largely assisting her with filing. However, before long, I realized how much I missed helping children.

Early on, I felt rather "child-like" during an unlikely experience occurring the first time the Rehab Center's van for handicapped people came to pick me up for the first time. I heard it coming, and went outside to get on the van. "Is this 2402 N. Willis?" the driver asked. "No, it is 2404 N. Willis." They had given him the wrong address, or perhaps he wrote it down wrong. He asked if I was Jan Eastland? "Yes," I answered. "Are you sure?" he questioned. By that time, I wasn't even sure I wanted to get on the van! What gives with this goober, I wondered.

A block or so later, he asked another lady -- guess she was a regular rider -- to look at my driver's license to make sure I was Jan Eastland. I played the scene out, and the lady told him I was indeed the person I claimed to be. It was a nightmare I did not wish to repeat. I knew deceased people sometimes were identified by a driver's license, but I always thought "live ones" could get by confirming their names verbally, or producing a document for proof. It was a mess. Upon arrival at work, I told Jerry what had happened to me. She burst into laughter, realizing immediately what had happened. The driver was under the mistaken impression I was a patient! I had to laugh, too….

Another similar experience occurred after I had been riding to work with another driver for a period of time. Turns out, he, too, assumed I was a patient, one day asking, "How long have you been coming to the Rehab Center." Deciding to "play along," I answered, "All of my life. I couldn't walk or talk when I first came." Kent responded, "Wow!" and he started thinking of me as a walking miracle.

Mr. Shelley Smith found me a place working with Gladys Hume in the History Center of the WTRC. Soon I was assigned to clipping articles about WTRC. They were to be assembled in notebooks to be placed in the Gladys Hume History Center of WTRC with her. It was a long process, since some of the articles went back to the days before the Rehab Center opened. It is quite interesting. These notebooks go back to the date when the Rehab Center was just getting started. I also typed index cards so folks looking at the material could easily find articles of particular interest to them. Dr. Aston, an HSU professor, put the notebooks on microfilm. It may be accessed in the HSU Library and at WTRC.

Bubba was another WTRC figure I'd place in the "nut" category, adding, in his case, that he's a "fruitcake" as well. Despite the fact that I love him dearly, I admit to calling him an "idiot" many times. But it was always in fun. He was forever shaking me until my teeth almost came loose, and upon seeing him, I always wondered, "Now how is Bubba planning to torment me today?"

In all seriousness, though, he really "lit up" the place. He did much to make the place both lively and interesting. When he left to pursue other employment, he left a large void behind. There was only one "Bubba."

Another worker, Nancy, likewise, was a mess, and she had a twin sister as ornery as she was. They must have been "double trouble" during their growing-up years. I'm not sure where they fit in the "nut" family. I guess "peanuts" will have to do.

One day, I entered Nancy's office, carrying my briefcase with all of my school papers in it. "I'm going to tell everyone over the intercom that you are carrying your dirty underwear in your briefcase," she threatened. Tease that she was, I didn't doubt it one bit. I told her to "Shut Up!," but this made no difference to her. It was something like this every time I saw her; she would have been bored if she hadn't had me to pick on.

Then John Thomas appeared on the scene. He was just like Bubba, and until him, I simply didn't think this was possible. Clearly, here was another "fruitcake." He picked on me every bit as much as Bubba did. I loved him, even though he was such a nut. Then I recall another who gave me grief. His name was Larry Farr. Let's just "ditto" him, however, and move on to other topics. He likes to shake me up, too.

I have repeatedly mentioned my deep appreciation and admiration for the folks at Rice Springs Care Home, Inc., in Haskell. They provided such loving care for my mother. As time rolled on, though, her health worsened. She was admitted to Hendrick Medical Center in Abilene, where she died on February 19, 1989, again, lovingly attended by doctors and nurses there.

Seeing her suffer was hard on me. She refused to eat in the final days, and along the way, gangrene set in. Her funeral was held at Haskell First Baptist Church on February 22, 1989, with Dr. Julian Bridges, Brother Pat Correll and Brother Jim Turner conducting the service. It was a beautiful service, and she was buried in Willow Cemetery.

Again, Haskell friends rose to the occasion to be of service. Eula Mae Herren opened her home to friends and relatives, and her many friends provided a covered dish luncheon for loved ones and friends.

During my second phase of work at WTRC, I became a member of the Human Relations Committee. We fought for minority rights, always seeking ways to make life better for them. Our major efforts were to widen job opportunities for them without regard to race, color, sex, national origin or handicaps. We sought to highlight awareness of human dignity as well. I am thankful that Dr. Bridges gave me opportunity to be on this committee, and was humbled to be the first handicapped person to serve on this committee. Always, yes always, we sought for levelling of the "playing field of life," including changes in the justice system, starting at the local level.

At our annual Martin Luther King, Jr. luncheon, we gave awards to Abilene employees who best exemplified principles of hiring without regard to race, color, sex, national origin or handicap. Also awarded was the "Worker of the Year With a Disability," again recognizing the same parameters. Finally, we also provided an award for the outstanding con-tributions of an individual or organization best demonstrating recognition of human dignity and worth.

The following articles appeared in the *Abilene Reporter-News*:

Stars Help Raise $1 Million
by Rebecca Harris

Once again the West Texas Rehabilitation Center has brought the stars to town, and the stardust fell to benefit the patients of the Rehab Center. This year almost $1 million was raised. Among those who work hard while they're here are Bill and Susan Hayes, who several years ago were soap operas most popular couple. They've been performing at the telethon for 16 years.

At the traditional party at Casa Herrera Friday night for the stars and other friends of the Rehab, Laurie Stevens, who handles the telethon pub-licity, told Bill and Susan they would be working especially hard this year.

She named the extra time they'd be on camera, the tapings they'd do, and the "extra" efforts they'd make for the Rehab Center. "You'll be really busy," Laurie warned. "We're here to help." Bill said. While they were eating, visited their tables and gave words of encouragement to the couple.

"We'll really miss you on "'Days of Our Lives,'" one fan said. I'm com-ing back," Susan said. She'll be returning the end of January, playing the richest woman on the show, a part she is going to relish.

Years ago, when skillet-playing virtuoso Pedro Gonzales began com-ing to the Rehab Telethon, he felt alone as "the only Mexican in sight."

Now I'm having dinner with Liz Herrera. Councilwoman Liz Herrera. That is better. I told Liz, next time maybe she'll be mayor.

I'm great with politicians," Pedro Said. "I've worked with Henry Cisneros, Henry Gonzales, and I've have made a movie with Ronald Reagan. Remember him?" If Liz needs me to campaign for her, I'll be ready."

Pedro got an endorsement of sorts from U.S. Rep. Charlie Stenholm, D-Stamford. They arrived at Abilene Regional Airport at the same time. While Charlie recognized Pedro, Pedro didn't recognize Charlie.

Television reporters were handling both interviews at once. Charlie told them: "If ya'll have any questions about the U.S. government, just ask Pedro."

Everybody has a favorite Rehab Telethon performer like Shari Lewis, Rex Allen, Anacani, and please make room for Gary Morris What a talent, what a voice! And Abilene can claim credit for his beginning, since his first professional gig was at Old Abilene Town while he was a student at Cisco Junior College.

The late Slim Willett and his music inspired the crafting of a massive stained glass window by Abilene artist Chris McCasland. Slim, the performer who organized country musicals at Fair Parks in the 50s, gained fame with his composition. "Don't Let The Stars Get In Your Eyes."

Chris' work features a starry Texas sky, yellow roses, cotton bolls, a longhorn skull and other Texas icons as the centerpiece. At the Petroleum Club where it was displayed, the setting sun streamed through the 19th floor windows, setting off the jeweled glass of a half-dozen large works, several windows and one door. The starry night piece, however, was the most spectacular. The work has 813 pieces of glass, 200 of them painted and fired. Some 145 yards of copper foil were used to bind the glass pieces.

Slim Willett's boots, red with yellow roses are represented in the center of the window. Butch Thorn, Chris' partner, explained that they bought two pair of Slim's boots at a flea market. The other pair was yellow with red roses. Even though it wasn't specifically indicated, I am sure much of the auctioned work benefited the Rehab Center. Among the hundreds or so guests at the reception were Chris' fans and patrons, among them being Dawn Wylie, Cindy and Mary Jane Moore, Marsha King, Dr. Ruth Ackers, Marshal and Karen Newcomb, Maxine Cockrell, Sue and Robert Patterson, Evelyn Fields, Margie Wells, Lindsay Minter, Marjorie Sayles and Frances Murphy.

Smith's Spirit Adds Inspiration to Rehab's Joint Venture Show

By Bob Lapham, Arts & Entertainment Editor
Abilene Reporter-News

Somehow, you knew Shelley Smith wouldn't miss the 1990 West Texas Rehabilitation Center Joint Venture for Children Thursday evening, despite his body being wracked by disease. Maybe the upcoming auction of oil field machinery, maybe the Cattlemen's Roundup or perhaps Shelley's personal "baby," the telethon next January must be held without his being present. Sure enough, a few hours later, the ravages of disease still his big heart, one that beat to serve the WTRC, which he founded 40 years earlier.

Shelley was there only in spirit for his final fund-raiser, "A Star-Spangled Evening with Lee Greenwood." But before Greenwood's moving encore presentation of "God Bless the U.S.A."—and sometime after his moving rendition of "The Wind Beneath My Wings," which he specifically dedicated to Smith—the WTRC founder passed from this life. His big, beautiful heart would beat no more.

Along about the time Greenwood crooned "It Turns Me Inside Out," he had his audience with him. Then came "Dixie Road," "I.O.U." and a really polished stage show.

He played guitar, keyboards and two different saxophones. He wandered into the audience, shaking hands with numerous guests, teased young lovers and applauded a couple who had been married 47 years. He involved the band more than most headliners, mentioning several times that his efforts were dedicated to the life of Shelley Smith. Not until the show was over did he, or most members of the audience, know that Smith had died. In the twinkling of an eye, Smith was in a better place.

REHAB'S SMITH DIES FROM HEART AILMENT
By Patrick Shaughnessy and Julie Anderson, Staff Writers

Thursday night, country-western singer Lee Greenwood was on stage at the Civic Center giving a performance to raise money for Shelley Smith's beloved West Texas Rehabilitation Center.

But Smith couldn't be there--he was in a Dallas hospital fighting for his life.

As Greenwood performed, however, Smith's fight came to an end. Smith, the only executive director the Rehab Center has had, died about 10 p.m. Thursday, succumbing to a series of heart attacks that had virtually destroyed his heart.

Smith was hospitalized July 9 after suffering the initial heart attacks. He was transferred to Baylor University Medical Center July 11 to be evaluated for a possible heart transplant. His condition did not improve.

Wednesday afternoon he took a turn for the worse, however, and his heart stopped, a hospital spokeswoman said. Emergency surgery was performed Wednesday night and a temporary device was implanted to help his heart keep going.

At 10 a.m., Thursday, he was taken in for additional surgery to stop internal bleeding. Twelve hours later he died.

Smith, 61, leaves behind a rich legacy in the Rehab Center, an institution that has improved the lives of thousands since he helped found it 37 years ago.

"You just can't say enough about the dedication that Shelley had for the West Texas Rehab Center," said Stormy Shelton, Chairman of the Rehab Foundation and publisher of the Reporter-News. I don't believe anyone has been more dedicated to the handicapped than Shelley," Shelton said. "Because of his dedication, there are many people living happy, productive lives."

"He's been such a key example of what Abilene stands for in so many ways, serving the people and his spirit of volunteerism," said an obviously shaken Mayor Gary McCaleb, who had just returned from the Joint Venture at the Civic Center. "It is a sad night for the people of West

Texas," McCaleb said. "But he has had such a full life and he's helped so many people."

When Smith came to Abilene almost 40 years ago, the West Texas Rehabilitation was little more than a dream, a plan to help the handicapped people of West Texas. He was the Rehab's only physical therapist, when it was founded in a wing of Bonham Elementary School on Aug. 15, 1953. His wife, Shirley, was the center's special education teacher. A maid completed the three-member staff, initially serving 17 patients.

But through Smith's efforts, the Rehab Center grew. His hard work helped expand services from a small operation in the wing of a school to a rehabilitation center that has touched and improved thousands of lives.

"Shelley was a unique individual," said Ken Murphy, president of the Rehab Center. "Fellows like him don't come around too often. We're going to miss him and always honor what he built and keep it going."

Smith, a native of Georgetown, came to Abilene in 1953 a year after receiving a certificate for physical therapy from Hermann Hospital School of Physical Therapy in Houston. He came from San Angelo, where he was director of the San Angelo Crippled Children Society.

From the beginning, he saw potential the infant Rehab Center held. "A rehab center for all handicapped and for all races and financial status was not a pipe dream; not really a dream; but a plan," he said in a 1978 interview. "Dreams are intangible; plans are solid," he claimed. "Any plans we have for tomorrow are built on sold foundations. We look for the needs of the future by using our best ability and using the past as a guide with lots of faith for the future." But, he knew if the center was to reach its potential, it needed the support of the community.

"You have to have money to buy bodies to take care of people," he said in 1978. "We're here for one reason: to rehabilitate the handicapped. I believe we should have heroes. And we're going to have winners and losers. And we're going to have the handicapped. If there is a medical need, that's all that's necessary," he said.

The center grew. In 1958, the Rehab Center began assisting the speech and hearing therapy program at Abilene Christian College. In

September 1973, a consortium for the training of speech pathology and audiology students was signed with ACC, HSU and the Rehab Center.

With the growth of the center, Smith's responsibilities also expanded. In 1967, he was appointed vice chairman of the Regional Coordinating Committee for statewide-planning aimed at comprehensive vocational rehabilitation programs and closure of the gap between the number of disabled who need services and the number who receive them.

In 1975, Smith was elected chairman of the Texas Education Agency's Advisory Council to the Office of Education for the Deaf, North Region.

In March 1986, Smith was named to a three-member task force to study physical therapy needs of clients of the Texas Department of Mental Health and Mental Retardation, representing the Parent Association for the Retarded of Texas. As recently as last month, Smith was appointed by Lt. Gob. Bill Hobby to the Office for the Prevention of Developmental Disabilities.

Smith's work was not unnoticed. Over the years he won many awards and honors, not only locally, but also regionally and nationally as well.as community.

In May 1961, Smith was named winner of the Mental Health award at the annual banquet of the Abilene Association of Mental Health. In March 1975, Shelley and Shirley Smith were honored at ACU as a couple who "have done God's service." The two were honored as a part of "Shelley and Shirley Smith Day" on the ACC campus. In 1977, he received an honorary doctorate from ACU.

In May of this year, District 44 Toastmasters named Shelley Smith as its 1990 Communication and Leadership Award winner during its spring conference. This is the organization's highest award made to an individual outside the organization.

"Shelley Smith is chosen not only for his exemplary contributions to West Texas, but also for his ability to lead in the tremendous growth of this very worthwhile endeavor," said Stan Black, co-chairman of the event. Smith was a member of the board of directors of the National Foundation of Infantile Paralysis, and also held membership in the American Registry of Physical Therapy and the Rotary

Club. He was a deacon at the Westgate Church of Christ. He also was a member of the American Academy for Cerebral Palsy. He served as vice president of the Abilene Council for Retarded Children and has served as full-time physical therapist for Taylor County Crippled Children's Society.

◆　◆　◆

Shelley Smith was a gifted man in many ways and had the ability to persuade celebrities like Bob Hope and many other entertainers to donate their talents to the annual fund-raising telethons and to other fund-raising events. Mr. Smith's expressed philosophy in conversation with friends, patients, and donors emphasized helping neighbors "in time of need." He believed this with all of his heart. Despite being a very busy man and shouldering the many responsibilities of leading the WTRC, he retained the personal touch. He was always available to talk with patients coming in for treatment, as well as with staff, stars, visitors and me. He was always happy to see me.

It did not matter who you were. I always thought that was neat. He always cared so much about everyone -- including the handicapped. He probably killed himself as he "over-worked" himself to death. Few persons would have cared that much.

The statistics of Mr. Shelley Smith's life speak for themselves. However, I would very much like to tell you what he meant to me personally. Our special relationship began in 1959, ending with his death. It was a relationship I find difficult to put into words. He was simply one of the most genuinely caring men I've ever known. He blessed my life, and those of many others, always with the support and assistance of his lovely wife, Shirley. He had little time for himself, and his sweet wife, Shirley--the kind so often described as being behind every successful man.

Shelley Smith married Shirley Sowell on in Cleburne, Texas on July 4, 1956. She is such a sweet person, and the kind one would figure he would select for his wife. They have two fine sons, Seth and Vance. They also have grandchildren. Seth and Vance are successful young men.

At our annual Martin Luther King, Jr. luncheon, we gave awards to Abilene employees who best exemplified principles of hiring without regard to race, color, sex, national origin or handicap. Also awarded was the "Worker of the Year With a Disability," again recognizing the same parameters. Finally, we also provided an award for the outstanding contributions of an individual or organization best demonstrating recognition of human dignity and worth.

Newspaper articles

The West Texas Rehabilitation Center is one of a kind, because the money raised goes directly to the Rehab Center. Mr. Smith and I shared mutual admiration from the first time I met him. I think God sent him as another father figure to me.

The Rehab board gives a turkey to each staff member every year at our annual Christmas party. On one particular Christmas it snowed. Ice was everywhere, but Mr. Smith and his wife were out delivering turkeys to the staff. They couldn't find my apartment, but finally did, saying, "You sure are hard to find." They, also, visited me in my apartment one other time. I was so blessed to get to know them and blessed by knowing him.

His life was far more than statistics. He was loved and respected by everyone. The day of his death was the saddest in history of the WTRC. Nearly everyone at work that day had a hard time keeping their minds on their jobs. John Thomas' statement was a "fit" for all of us. "A piece of my heart died today."

Dr. and Mrs. Bridges were kind enough to invite me to attend the funeral with them. I did, and was very comforted to be in a huge crowd that love Shelley Smith like I did. Still, Shirley Smith carried on. Even during her grief, she prepared chicken and dumplings for me at a time when I had a sore on my tongue and could eat very little.

Mr. Smith endeared himself to many, and he was most persuasive. Rex Allen and Rex Allen, Jr., became important devotees to the WTRC. Allen described Smith as being "one of the world's greatest beggars!"

They made a sculpture of Mr. Smith's face. It has Mr. Smith's twinkle in his eyes -- he always had a twinkle in his eyes. The sculpture is located in the lobby of the West Texas Rehabilitation Center, near a great portrait of Mr. Smith. You can feel the love people still have for Shelley Smith. I always wanted a picture of Mr. and Mr. Smith. He agreed to give me one, but failed to do it before he died. In the meantime, Shirley has given me a picture of them, and it is a great picture.

Later, at a meeting of the Human Relations Committee, I was privileged to report that some grocery stores and department stores do not provide wheelchairs for their customers. In her opinion, this is a serious matter. A motion was made by Esperanza Rogers to send letters to area stores, encouraging the provision of wheelchairs for the wheelchair bound population. The motion, seconded by Ric Arnic, carried.

The upcoming annual telethon was discussed, and I prayed for the new director, Bill Snowden. At the event, we raised more than $1 million. Again, God -- as well as returning stars and several new ones -- shined on us.

Dr. and Mrs. Bridges were kind enough to invite me to attend the funeral with them. I did, and was very comforted to be in a huge crowd that loved Shelley Smith like I did. Still, Shirley Smith carried on. Even during her grief, she prepared chicken and dumplings for me at a time when I had a sore on my tongue and could eat very little.

Mr. Smith endeared himself to many, and he was most persuasive. Rex Allen and Rex Allen, Jr., became important devotees to the WTRC. Allen described Smith as being "one of the world's greatest beggars!"

They made a sculpture of Mr. Smith's face. It has Mr. Smith's twinkle in his eyes—he always had a twinkle in his eyes. The sculpture is located in the lobby of the West Texas Rehabilitation Center, near a great portrait of Mr. Smith.

You can feel the love people still have for Shelley Smith. I always wanted a picture of Mr. and Mrs. Smith. He agreed to give me one, but failed to do it before he died. In the meantime, Shirley has given me a picture of them, and it is a great picture.

The following articles appeared in the Abilene Reporter News:

"Rehab 91" New and Old Stars Shine at Annual Telethon
--By BOB LAPHAM
Arts & Entertainment Editor

Holly Dunn "used to read up on what was happening " at the annual West Texas Rehabilitation back when she was enrolled at ACU. Saturday night, the 1979 ACU graduate finally got to see what was happening. She was finally getting her degree in advertising from ACU. She was behind the bright lights to the "picture line," getting her picture made with fans seeking autographs.

By midnight, $ 1,020,012 had been raised for the Rehab Center and pledges were still coming in. During Holly's first WTRC telethon, stars helping out included B.J. Thomas, Anita Bryant, and Karen Delong.

And, it might be added, Troy Aikman. The Dallas Cowboys' quarterback clearly was the favorite of the show. Fresh from surgery on his multi-million dollar right elbow, Aikman drew a standing ovation from the near-packed house at Abilene Civic Center. And he drew the longest line at the photo booth, where for $5 (minimum) per Polaroid shot, Aikman posed patiently with each of his fans while Bill and Susan Hayes were holding down their usual spot at the annual Rehab Auction across the hall perennial co-hosts Rx Allen and Shari Lewis geared up the latest Rehab that was dedicated to the memory of Shelley Smith, its founder and guiding light until his death almost six months ago. The show was telecast live on satellite network of 11 stations in Texas and Oklahoma, anchored by KRBC.

Thomas was the opening act, and he set the tone for the night by singing "The Impossible Dream" to honor Smith's memory. It was the first time the Dallas resident had performed the show standard.

Bill Snowden, well-known therapist and aid to his cousin before succeeding Smith as the executive director, introduced the founder's family – Shirley Smith and her two sons, Seth and Vance. Snowden also introduced Abilene sculpture Terry Galbraith, who has been commissioned to do a bronze busts of Smith, two of which will be cast for WTRC's Abilene and San Angelo campuses. Galbraith showed the clay master, which is well on its way to completion.

Allen crouched before the piece and nodded. "Yep, that is the greatest beggar in the world," he said, going back to his description of his longtime friend. "He has got that little smile on his face (in the sculpture)."

"Shelley's dream is going to live on for a long time," Mrs. Smith said, responding to accolades for her late husband. "(The sculpture) will be a wonderful tribute."

Outgoing and incoming president of the WTRC board of directors Myrle Greathouse and David Stubbeman, respectively, along with Dr. Tom Burditt and State Rep. Bob Hunter (R-Abilene) assisted in kicking off the telethon and its dedication.

Lewis, always a hit at the Rehab with her sidekick, hand puppet Lamb Chop was in usual high form. She explained to Lamb Chop how great it was, doing something useful to help WTRC raise some of the $7 million it will need this year to serve more than 13,000 cases of handicapped referred by more than 750 physicians.

"Who's less handicapped than me?" Lamb Chop demanded to know of her alter ego. "I'm only 16 inches tall, and every time I try to talk, you stick your hand up my..."

"All right. All right," the charming Lewis responded.

Bryant did a medley of her million-selling singles ("My Little Corner of the World, "Paper Roses" and "Till There was You.")

"I'm an Okie, but I've probably got more relatives in Texas than in Oklahoma," she said during her visit to Abilene.

Delong joined Thomas during the opening set to duet with him on "As Long As We've Got Each Other," his hit theme song from the TV show, "Growing Pains." The former beauty queen had to endure her hand mike failing for a couple of bars, "and that is the first time that ever happened to me," she said, backstage, "It' s a weird feeling."

Dunn's opening set was framed by her career-launching first hit single of four years ago, "Daddy's Hands," which she called "a salute to your dad and my dad," and to WTRC.

Dunn's father, Frank Dunn, is a Church of Christ minister (The University Hills Church) in Austin where he lives with his wife and Holly's mother, Yvonne. Holy credits her older brother (also an ACU graduate) with paving the way for her in Nashville, where he still lives and works in the entertainment business.

Backstage, she talked about the fast pace of life for one of Nashville's rising young stars. "Time off? "she responded. "I took four days off around Christmas and that was about it—for the entire year"

She has a new band ("I've got to keep busy—I have 14 family members depending on me"), a new album and a new chart-hot single on the Warner Bros. label called "Heartfull of Love," She said she has been given boost by two of Nashville's legends, Dolly Parton and Reba McEntire. Dunn said she associates her career particularly with McEntire's. "We have spent a lot of time in the dressing room the other night talking about things." Dunn said. "I write, produce, sing and take it on the road, much like McEntire." Dunn said Warner Bros. has given her virtually total control of her sessions and music selection. This is rare in country music—particularly for female stars.

She spent Wednesday rehearsing and setting up for her "Down Home" spot on the Grand Ole Opry TV show with the Gatlin Brothers and Friday's visitor to the Taylor County Coliseum, Alan Jackson.

The 65th Anniversary Show (Dunn became the 64th member of the Opry last year) was filmed Thursday by CBS for telecast later this month. Less than 24 hours later, she and her band and entourage had taken their "glorified mobile home" to Oklahoma for an appearance. Then it was straight through to Abilene, rehearsal for Rehab Saturday afternoon, and the show that night. Other Rehab stars and performers Saturday included Rex Allen Jr., dancer Arthur Duncan (along with special guests from Abilene's Patty Harper Dance studio), singer Anacani (with Duncan, once a member of the Lawrence Welk TV show ensemble), the Maines Brothers Band, the Medders Sisters, the Reinsman Band, Dr. Ed George directing the always-impressive Rehab Orchestra, R&D Do R&B, Abilenians Roy Sharp and Doug LoPachin, actor Pedro Gonzales Gonzales and the St. Vincent's Ballet Folklorico.

Stars Shine for Crowd at Rehab '92
By Bob Lapham
Arts & Entertainment Editor

The stars were out Saturday night at Abilene Civic Center. Anita Bryant once again and conquered the Rehab '92 crowd, Rex Allen Sr. was given a surprise honor, Lorrie Morgan was kept under tight security and the Big Country welcomed one of its own, Brad Maule, to the telethon's spotlight.

The 22nd annual major fund-raiser for the West Texas Rehabilitation beamed its five-hour show via satellite and 11-station hook-up to a good part of Texas, Oklahoma, and New Mexico. Once again $1 million was the unofficial target for pledges.

Bryant, the co-host and entertainment's iron woman of career adversity, seems to have nothing but friends in the Big Country. She co-hosted with Allen in a role that seems to be made for her in the future. Bryant put an army fatigue over her glittering blue evening gown and for the second straight year, stopped the show with "Battle Hymn of the Republic."

The jacket had been given to her by a soldier in Vietnam, shortly before he was killed in battle. She wore it on all her all her trips to entertain troops. It was covered with "insignias from all over and private's patches to a general's star (Gen. William Westmoreland's) she had collected on her travels with Bob Hope.

Earlier in the day, a prayer breakfast featuring Bryant had been sold out for almost 48 hours. Bryant's and gay rights activists battled a couple of year ago in a well-publicized war that lasted for several years, effectively shutting down the former Oklahoma beauty queen's career. Last year, there was a small gay right's picket at the Civic Center. This year, none was noticed.

Allen predates the "modern" Rehab, begun in 1971, by several years, in both telethon work and Cattlemen's Roundup for Crippled Children. Unknown to him, a bronze sculpture of the former movie singing cowboy and his legendary horse, Koko, had been struck and brought from Arizona to Abilene to for permanent placement at the center.

Allen was brought on stage while a video of his early movie clips and songs was shown. WTRC board chairman and former Abilene mayor David Stubbemen presented the bronze. Bill Snowden, executive director of Rehab told Allen, "When I was a kid, I used to go to the old Ritz Theater in Georgetown where my favorite singing cowboy was Rex Allen. Little did I know that someday, I'd be here with him."

Rex Allen, Jr. serenaded his father with a song he penned "Last of the Silver Screen Cow boys," as Rex Sr. took off the tinted glasses and dabbed at his eyes. The senior Allen was still moved when he made his way backstage. "I feel like I just went to my own funeral, " he said, somberly.

Morgan sang half a dozen songs early in the show, backed by her traveling group, the Slam Band. She was canceling most other appearances that normally go with Rehab. When she did leave her dressing room, she was flanked shoulder to shoulder by two aides and trailed by two uniformed policemen. Word was that the pretty blond country star remained shaken by a recent "crowd incident" at another engagement.

Maule grew up on a family stock farm near Camp Springs and was educated through high school at nearby Snyder. For eight years he has played the popular Dr. Anthony Jones on the daytime ABC soap opera "General Hospital." Last year, the singer-songwriter released an album of country songs he had written.

Maule arrived in Abilene only a couple of hours before the telethon, and had time for just one quick run-through of his program with the slick Maines Brother Band of Lubbock. He opened with "Mamma Blue," and after he sang the last line, "I couldn't stand to think of makin' Mamma blue," he nodded and said, "That's for you, Mamma."

Maule's parents, George and Josie Maule, still work the family stock farm near Camp Springs. The 1950 Snyder high graduate's program also included and upbeat ditty called, "Cut Me, and I Bleed Country."

Bill and Susan Hayes, who go back with Rehab almost as far as Allen, arrived in time to help push quilts, donated for the Rehab auction. Susan was seen live on national TV less than 24 hours earlier as one of the featured presenters in the annual "Soap Opera Digest Awards." Her show, "Days of Our Lives," was particularly strong in grabbing awards.

"We won in every major category except one," she said proudly, in between signing autographs and talking to fans. Miss Texas, Ronda Morrison, held court Saturday, especially at the photo booth. Fiddler Jonna Fitzgerald and singer Karol Ann Delong, both former beauty queens themselves, also performed. Anacani, the beautiful former featured singer for Lawrence Welk, and ex-Welk dancer Arthur Duncan, returned; as did movie character actor Pedro Gonzalez Gonzalez. Dr. Ed George and his Rehab Band were well received. Abilene Christian University's Vocal Jazz Ensemble helped them add extra class to the show.

❖ ❖ ❖

LIVING THE DREAM *for 38 Years, Attorney Fred Gray has Litigated for Civil Rights of All Men*

Tuskegee, Alabama -- Over the telephone, you can hear car horns outside attorney Fred Gray's office. You might think a giant in civil rights such as Gray would occupy a room with a quieter view.

But the civil rights movement, while not violent, certainly was not quiet. And as its leader of the Martin Luther King, Jr., was a simple man, and so is Gray, who has spoken before the Supreme Court of the United States and spoken before small church congregations on Sunday mornings. Gray is doing that this morning, at Abilene's Minda Street Church of Christ. At 1 p.m. he joins 1,000 others at the first King Awards Luncheon at the Abilene Civic Center.

In 1954, the 20 year-old recent law school graduate returned to his home state of Alabama. Though advised to stay in Cleveland, Ohio, where he attended law school at Case Western Reserve, and earn a good living, the Montgomery, Ala. native chose to go home to work for his people.

It wasn't long before they came knocking at his door. Rosa Parks, a seamstress at a downtown department store, tired after a long day on her feet, refused to give up her seat to a white man on a crowded Montgomery city bus. She was arrested on Dec. 1, 1955, and Gray was asked to defend her.

With that simple demonstration of human dignity, the civil rights movement began with it early leader King, now in charge of Bower vs. W.A. Gayle, the mayor of Montgomery, segregation of races on city buses was found unconstitutional. The bus protest was ended.

Gray since has been the defense attorney in the courtroom when many of the far reaching civil rights cases of this century have heard, argued, and decided.

NAACP vs. State of Alabama (1958)—Decided by the Supreme Court, the NAACP-- outlawed in the state of Alabama--was unable to resume activities.

G.G. Comillion, et al vs. Mayor of Tuskegee (1960) –Landmark case in that it laid the foundation for the redistricting and reapportionment of the state legislature.

Vivian Malone vs. Dean of Admissions, University of Alabama (1963 -- A simple desegregation case on behalf of student Anthony and Henry Lee resulted in a statewide order requesting desegregation of all public elementary and secondary schools; desegregation of trade and junior colleges; desegregation of all instructions of higher learning; merger of Alabama Athletic Association white) and Alabama Interscholastic Athletic Association (black); integration of public school faculty and staff.

Additionally, Gray handled cases upholding tenure for all public school teachers, acquitted a black sheriff and his chief deputy, dismissed charges against three ministers—including King--charged with violating anti-boycott statue and ordered statewide repetition of the same thing. Gray was still righting wrongs in 1970 when the facilities of the Montgomery YMCA were integrated.

Gray, who turns 61 this year, is the senior partner of Gray, Langford. Sapp, McGowan & Gray (Fred, Jr. his son; another son, Stanley, also is an attorney). He looks back 38 years to those tumultuous days and admits, "the years have run very rapidly."

Presently he is working on a book covering these historic events as seen for the first time through the eyes and mind of an attorney. "I was doing what I wanted to do," he says of the tasks facing a young law school graduate. "The opportunity really appeared and all the pieces just fell in place much quicker than I had ever imagined. And from one thing to another, it just has never stopped." "I did not start out with any intention of making history. I saw a condition that needed to be changed…things could be different. That motivating factor took me into law school and my intention was to come back to my community to change things. As we began to change things, I recognized history was being made. (The intent) was to do what we could and it just developed." "As we moved along, I received opportunities to handle precedent-setting cases. "

The developments included a personal friendship with King, who in his book. Stride Toward Freedom, calls Gray "the brilliant young Negro who later became the chief council for the protest movement." And a relationship with a circuit court judge named Wallace who later became governor and tried, physically, to bar black students from the University of Alabama.

George Wallace 's racist attorney, Gray explains, emerged after running not as a racist and losing an early legislative race against John Patterson. Gray prefers to recall Wallace's prior character.

"He did start out as a racist," Gray recalls. "He was as fair to me in the way he treated me and conducted the trials as any judge I had appeared before. " But Wallace changed, and it was change for the worse. Now he admits he did a lot of things wrong in connection with the whole race issue. He definitely has changed." Gray, in an ironic stroke of justice, represented Wallace's county (Barbour) in the state legislature, 1970-74, as one of the first two blacks elected since Reconstruction. King, Gray emphasizes, did not seek leadership of the movement, which organized after the Parks arrest.

At that time, the leadership in Montgomery included E.D. Nixon, a local labor movement leader whose wife was a member of Gray's church, and Rufus Lewis, a coach at Alabama State University where Gray earned his bachelor's degree.

Nixon—whom Gray calls "Mr Civil Rights For Everything"—early on led planning of the bus boycott in 1955, getting support from a young Baptist preacher named Ralph Abernathy. Lewis' interest was primarily in voting rights in part because he operated The Citizens Club, a nightclub which admitted only persons who were registered voters.

Choosing one man over the other as leader, Gray recalls, "We would lose some of the other's followers. The question was who we could get to effectively serve as spokesman was what we called our initial efforts.

"(King) had come to Montgomery about the same time I had returned home to practice law," Gray recalls, describing the young minister as articulate, well spoken, and easy-going. "He never spoke any violent words, had a command of the English language and could really move people, " Gray says. "People see Martin as the international person that he became. He didn't come to be a national hero or a civil rights leader, and he was not a civil rights leader prior to the movement. He had not been involved locally...in any civil rights activities. "He was selected to lead the movement as a means of bringing the community together.

No one actually went out looking for Martin Luther King to lead the movement...the pieces just fell into place. "And I think today, if we go around looking for someone to lead African Americans, we are going to be sadly mistaken." Having worked with and walked beside King, Gray loyally believes there never will be a man of similar "charisma and command that warrant both leadership and fellowship. " "I doubt it very seriously," he says. "People like that aren't made, so to speak." It's the circumstances, and I think the Lord had something to do with it. They emerged." King was assassinated in Memphis. Tenn., in 1968 and this year will mark the 25th anniversary of that tragic event. Where has the Civil Rights movement marched since?

Gray prefaces his answer by saying that indeed much has been accomplished. "A lot of good has happened since Sept. 14,1954, when I was admitted to practicing law," he says. "Everything at that time in Alabama and throughout the South was segregated based on race, and sanctioned by law. Many of those barriers have been changed."

Alas, Gray continues, the highpoints seem to be in the past; today, the forward direction of the movement has been stopped. Young blacks, as shown dramatically in movies by the new generation of black film-makers, are angry. "I think there's a senses of frustration because of the lack of opportunity to get and continue in meaningful jobs. " Gray says. "Particularly in the minority communities." "So many youngsters have absolutely nothing to do, and would be gainfully employed if they could find something to do. Once they don't have the jobs, they get involved in a lot of problems and activities. They have time on their hands with noth-ing to do and then somebody will come by and show them how they can make a whole lot of money quickly, like selling drugs. "

And for all minorities, Gray says, "We still have racism and discrimi-nation." So-called equal opportunity employers, he says, still will hire a Caucasian 90 percent of the time, even if minority applicants are equally qualified for the job." Gray backs the statement by noting a recent case concluded in April of last year, in which a federal district judge, in a 850-page opinion, found "vestiges of racial discrimination" still in higher education in Alabama. While strides have been made politically, "eco-nomically, we are at the bottom of the totem pole," he says. "It's there, it's subtle, and it's more difficult to attack than before." Blacks he says once looked to the federal court system to bring about change. Gray views today's court alignment as not at all sympatric to minorities. "Now we have a court of young, articulate, male, Caucasian and brilliant ultra-conservative judges who do not see the problems and solutions the way that (Warren) court judges did 25 years ago," Gray says. "They are mak-ing findings of facts and conclusions of law that are really turning the clock back. We have had a Congress ...pass legislation to reverse the decisions of the Supreme Court, which is the reverse of the way you used to have to do it. We depended on the Supreme Court to be our salvation, and now it's the other way." Though Gray's tone sounds dishearten, he isn't. "By nature, I am an optimist," he said recently in the Case Western Reserve University magazine. "I think we have just got to keep working. We're going to have setbacks, we're going to have disappointments. But that's part of the struggle. We have to keep going."

❖   ❖   ❖

February 10, 1992
Earl Williams, Chair and members of the
Human Relations Committee

Dear Earl and Committee Members,
The Martin Luther King luncheon is one of the most memorable events that I have ever experienced. The closest I can come to describing the excitement and feeling of being a part of something bigger than all of us was the All-American City Award.
I am very honored by your recognition –but there is such a hand-in-glove partnership between you as Committee members and myself as staff. I know you recognize we have all worked hard as Committee and staff to build a team and it is the lifeblood of the good we have been able to accomplish together. With Earnest Merritt on board, our team will be doubly enriched. More simply, I don't deserve the award but I don't mind it hanging on my wall where people can see it as a symbol of the values we share. I'll tell you another thing I'm very proud of, and that is that very seldom do people at City Hall in any city get recognized for working on behalf of human and minority relations. The two seem sometimes to be mutually exclusive goals.
On a more personal note, the award has been a great inspiration on a daily basis to do a better job of encouraging the development of the full potential of people around me in all areas I get involved. There was a lot of teambuilding and community

building going on behind the scenes of the luncheon. I feel we all learned a little more about our potential to really effect change and make a difference in Abilene, Texas. The experiences of working and having fun with the HRC are a rich part of my life. Some of my favorite moments were....

* *Kathy's and Tony's faces when they first learned that the event night was a sellout;*
* *Jan Eastland's voice describing how excited she was to be able to name the winners;*
* *the TV news that night as the camera rolled over the crowd—the size and multi-ethnicity of everyone there . . . what an event!*
* *hearing the multicultural youth choir and seeing my kids....*

   .....nowhere else but Abilene...

   Thanks for letting me share such a powerful moment in history in January 1992.

   Sincerely,

   Debra S. Guerra

❖   ❖   ❖

The following is information discussed in a meeting of the Human Relations Committee in 1994. It included discussion concerning speaker selection for the Martin Luther King Jr. awards luncheon for 1995:

It was decided there would be three speakers, with invitations extended to Lynda Calcote, Robert Chris and Jorge Solis.

Other discussion concerned the need for mobile wheelchairs at the mall. Members Jan Eastland and Julian Bridges were asked to meet with mall officials, with the item to be discussed at the July meeting.

Following, Chief of Police Melvin Martin spoke about hiring practices of the Police Department, emphasizing the community-policing concept and dependence on the Citizens' Police Academy. He announced plans for organizing a Teen Police Academy in the fall, and appealed for help in recruiting minority candidates for the next class of the Police Academy. It was evident that concern for minority consideration was growing.

I was privileged to report that some grocery stores and department stores do not provide wheelchairs for their customers. In her opinion, this is a serious matter. A motion was made by Esperanza Rogers to send letters to area stores, encouraging the provision of wheelchairs for the wheelchair bound population. The motion, seconded by Rick Arnic, carried.

I am still on the local Human Relations Committee. We are still trying to help minority people every way we can. We deal with many problems. I am trying to be sensitive to the needs of my handicapped colleagues.

Target Stores has a special shopping day for the handicapped people during the Christmas holidays. We sent a letter in recognition of that. We were able to get wheelchairs in every grocery store in town. We weren't able to get an electric wheelchair for the Mall of Abilene, but they do have push wheelchairs available for elderly and handicapped people. I am glad I have been given the opportunity to be able to help my fellow handicapped people in such ways.

As a member of the Human Relations Committee, I have met and worked with many wonderful people. A man challenged us to have a big celebration of the birthday of Martin Luther King, Jr. We accepted the challenge, but had no idea it would go over so big.

The first Martin Luther King Luncheon ran too long, but has been improved each year as we have learned from our mistakes. We had a wonderful speaker, Fred Gray, and had a huge youth choir made up of kids of all colors. I was privileged to announce names of the people and business to receive awards.

I was a member of the Indoor Sports Club for about twenty-five years, serving as Abilene Chapter President. We met monthly, always trying to help physically handicapped persons, plus enjoying the social aspects of meeting together.

Many years ago, the organization was instrumental in redoing sidewalks to make them accessible to handicapped persons trying to manipulate wheelchairs. Then, the organization successfully lobbied for more handicapped parking spaces. More recently, we have been successful in getting met once a month, and we were trying to help handicapped people, as well getting together socially once a month. We support each other. A long time ago the Indoor Sports Club got sidewalks leveled, so the wheelchairs could easily get up on sidewalks. We also advocated for the physically handicapped to have increased numbers of handicapped parking spaces. Recently, we have been successful in conversion of bathrooms at the Fair Ground so they can be accessible for persons in wheelchairs. We have conventions throughout the United States, and much progress is being made. We are extremely grateful for local leaders like Gladys and Bill Hume, whose work is genuinely appreciated.

Chapter 12

❖   ❖   ❖

LUCKY ENOUGH TO GO TO GEORGIA: CONTINUED WORK WITH HUMAN RELATIONS AND WTRC TELETHONS

My grandmother on my mother's side of the family came from Georgia many years ago. Helen and Jack Cobb live in Georgia. They are kinfolks who came to see us many years ago when I was a little girl. We did not see them for years, but my aunt kept in touch with exchange of letters.

Some 30 years ago, they came to see us. It was so much fun taking them all over Abilene, and even drove to San Angelo to see my aunt and uncle there. We made a bunch of pictures, and I fell in love with this wonderful couple.

Then, guess what? A few years later, I flew to Atlanta, George ALL BY MYSELF to visit them, and I found out what you may be anticipating. I found some more "nuts," and they were kin to me!

On the way from home, I made it fine -- until I reached the Dallas airport. It was too far to walk to the plane, so they put me in a wheelchair, and it was an odd feeling, strapped in the chair and the chair secured in the plane. I told the lady in the electric cart that I needed to go to Gate 33, and that was a mistake. Instead of ticketing me to Atlanta, they had me going to Amarillo! By the time the mistake was discovered, I'd missed my flight. They were "sorry about it," and got me on the next flight. They also called the Atlanta airport to tell my uncle and aunt that I would be on a later flight.

A nice handicapped lady was on the cart with me, and she stayed with me the whole time. We ate together in Dallas, and she made me feel much better. She stayed with me the whole time I was eating and talked to me. She also made me feel better. I thought that it was not just a mere coincidence that she was handicapped, too. It was as if God had planned it that way. She took me to the correct airplane, and even helped me get on the plane herself. I suppose because of the earlier error, they put me in first class. There I ate some more, watching others in the cabin drinking SOFT drinks instead of beer. That really made an impression on me!

I was as glad to see my kinfolks, as they were to see me. I had worried that they had not gotten the message about my delay, but they said it was the first thing they heard upon arrival at the airport. They have a neat subway at the Atlanta Airport, and, thanks to helpful new friends and my relatives on the other end, I had made my first flight alone. Jack and Helen took me to Roswell, Georgia, where I met their son, Craig, whom I like very much.

We rested a while the next day, and then we went to see the Great Smoky Mountains. They were gorgeous; Grandmother must have been "nuts" to leave such beautiful country to come to West Texas. It was indescribably beautiful. Then we went to Cleveland, Georgia, to see the Babyland General Hospital where the Cabbage Patch Kids are born. The "nurses" were dressed in white, just like in a real hospital. People were visiting there from everywhere. I wanted a Cabbage Patch Doll, but settled for a stuffed bear that was not so expensive.

The next day we drove to see a huge lake, and then on to Helen, Georgia, which is really Georgia's own "Alpine village." The city fathers recently had redone it into a beautiful little city. They are very proud of it. We went into local shops, all of which looked like shops in the towns and villages of Switzerland. We bought lots of picture post cards and books.

Then we drove to Cherokee, North Carolina, and it was something to see. Mama Sue came from South Carolina, but I never dreamed I'd ever get to go to North Carolina.

I learned that Georgia had been Indian country, and we saw big mounds where they had buried Indians. Then, we met Helen and Jack's daughter, Teresa, her husband, Pat, as well as their daughter Andrea and son Eric. (Pat has since died.)

It was Andrea's birthday, and we all had birthday cake. I also met some of Helen's other family members, and I spent a day with my cousin Marie, who has been ill. I also met her daughter Pat, and we enjoyed going to a couple of auctions.

On Saturday afternoon, we drove to Stone Mountain, and the whole family went. I enjoyed being with them. I had always wanted to see Stone Mountain, since I had heard of the old mountain all my life. We heard about its history, rode the train around it and took the lift to its summit. The memorial carving is something to see, and the light show is simply breath-taking. We didn't get home until 1 a.m., so we rested quite a bit the next day.

Sunday, we visited a big, beautiful shopping mall. It was my birthday, so I bought some clothes and a necklace, and my family gave me cards, a ring and Stone Mountain souvenirs. Tammy is a craft artist, and this is right down my alley. I love arts and crafts. She made he a bear and a beautiful George Peach T-shirt. Teresa gave me some beautiful cloths, and it was a birthday I'll never forget.

I determined that Jack is a "walnut," because he is so hard-headed. He caught himself on fire shortly before I got there, but he refused to go to the doctor until someone scared him into it. So, the possibility that he is an "acorn nut " remains. Their children are a cross between a "walnut" and an "acorn nut." They all have senses of humor and are fun to be with. They are unusual in that they call each other nicknames instead of their real names. Helen calls Jack names like "Corn Cob" and "Jack-O-Lantern" and "Peg Leg." Graig calls Teresa "Sister," and he calls his daddy "Jack-O-Lantern." Andrea calls Jack names like "Goofy" and "Bird Brain." Other nicknames include Meat Loaf, Meat Head, Knuckle Head and Goofy. They mean no disrespect, but are simply having fun. I laughed and laughed at them.

Then it was time to go home, and I didn't want to go. Jack, Helen and Andrea took me to meet my plane, and it was raining. I asked Helen, "Why does it have to be raining?" Andrea heard Jack and Helen say they would have to get me a wheelchair when we got to the airport. Andrea asked, "Why does Jan need a wheelchair? She is not retarded." I told Andrea that she was smarter than a lot of grown people. I thought what she said was so cute. When we got there my flight had been cancelled, so I had to wait again. They stayed with me until I ate my dinner. Then they left.

One sees a lot of interesting sights at airports, people dressed in many different ways. I did not have any problems at the Dallas Airport, and upon my arrival at Abilene Regional, Bob picked me up. Helen called me a while back and said, "I've just lost Jack." It made me sick; I had so wanted him to read my book. Helen said she had really been through the mill. She also asked, "Where have you been?" She had been trying to get me by phone for quite some time. I told her I was so sorry about Jack's death, and that I had been right here at home most of the time.

Not everyone is my life is a "nut," of course, although they are very important to me. Everyone' life, I believe, should include a a mixture of "nuts" who, really are not nuts, but with differences enough to make everyone unique, and sort of balance each other out. Mr. and Mrs. Shelley Smith and Mr. and Mrs. Charles B. Thornton, Charlotte Bridges, and Mr. and Mrs. Paul J. Williams are not assigned to any "nut" categories. Yet, they are the most important people in my life due to their dedication to God, as well as what God means to them regarding my life, and in other areas of life. They are truly giants in my eyes, and none of these men and women think they are great. Great men and women never do.

I cannot say enough about these precious men and women. I can say that each and every one of them love me and look after me every step of the way. If I did, I'd probably have to write another book. In fact, I may, anyway. I just haven't made up my mind yet. Selfish and self-centered people miss out on so many blessings, and I feel sorry for them. I regularly claim Luke 6:38, which says "Give and it will be given unto you. A good measure, pressed down, shaken together, and running over, will be poured into your lap. For with the measure you use, it will be measured to you." That is really true -- I have experienced this myself.

I am still working at the West Texas Rehabilitation Center, and I still enjoy it very much. Henry still works there, and he remains a "peanut." One day, he met me in the hall with Super Glue on his hands. He said, "Let me in the hall, and Henry said, "Let me put this Super Glue on your lips so you can use it as lipstick. Of course, I told him to "Shut Up."

Mr. Tucker works out there, too, and we pick on each other. Mr. Tucker is a deacon at the First Baptist Church of Abilene, but you would never know it from the way he acts. He told me one Christmas that he was going to wrap up a mouse in a box and give it to me for Christmas, then watch me have a heart attack. I told him to "Shut Up!" He is another "pecan nut." His daughter Cara works out there, too. She is a precious friend.

Another worker, Mr. Frymire loves to pick on me. Barbara Trusler is another fellow worker who gets so tickled at me. She always asks, "Are you behaving yourself?" I always respond, "No, I am not!" Then she answers, "I didn't think you were."

On the Rehab Van I ride to and from the Rehab Center, I rode with a woman for about six weeks. One day, sitting beside me, she asked, "Do you live at the house for retarded people?" I informed her, "No, I have a college degree." The woman said, "You are kidding!" I patiently said, "No, I'm afraid I am not kidding." I could have gotten mad at her, but I thought it was extremely funny. Now, I am not saying anything against retarded people in general, because they are precious people in the sight of God and to me. It is just that I wish people would learn that not every handicapped person is retarded. And, even retarded people have different levels of retardation. Some retarded people have some intelligence. They know when they are being mistreated.

Mr. Smith has been dead for sixteen years now. And we still miss him, and I suppose we always will. We are still having telethons and I am still on the Human Relations Committee. Still in attendance every year at the telethon, I never attend but that I think of Mr. Smith.

Chapter 13

❖ ❖ ❖

LIVING ON MY OWN

During the second phase of my WTRC days, I lived by myself while mother was in the rest home. I lived by myself for eight years, never thinking I could do so. I was able to dress and undress myself, and managed to get food prepared by people who cared about me, and would accept my paying for the food. I also managed to care for my dog, all the while working part-time at West Texas Rehab. Actually, it was more fun living by myself.

We have a City Link Bus for handicapped people; it takes people places and brings them home. My friends – Bob, John and Hazel – also help me with my transportation. I always enjoy getting out and doing things.

My adopted mom was a lot of help to me. My prayer partner, Charlotte, and I had been praying for a mother and her family with a cerebral palsied handicapped child or baby, because I thought that I could be a lot of help in helping them understand their child better. One day at the Rehab Center, while on the elevator with a mother, she was holding a cerebral palsy baby in her arms. She mentioned that I have cerebral palsy as well, and I confirmed it. A few days later, I went upstairs to run copies of my book manuscript off on the copy machine. I looked up, and there was the lady and part of her family. After introductions, I got her telephone number, and she wanted me to call her. About a week later, we had lunch together, and we had a good sharing session. We got together several times after that, then she wanted me to come home with her and meet her family.

Leon Johnson is her husband, and he is a "walnut," a real character. Linda is the mother, and Jared is the cerebral palsy baby. (He is now older) He had a premature birth. Darren and Kristi are his brother and sister. We all get along very well together. Linda and I still get together and have lunch. We also go to the movies. After dinner one night at their house, Leon said, "I guess you know we have a cat in our freezer." I couldn't imagine eating a cat for supper, then I realized it was a joke. I told him to "Shut Up!"

Then I started spending Christmas Eve with them. We sure had some fun times. I have really been a lot of help to Linda and her family. Linda also has twins, who are older, and they have families of their own.

Charlotte and Dr. Bridges spent a semester in China, where he was teaching. A while after that, one of his students from China came all the way by herself just to see them. She brought many gifts with her. When he wasn't working, the Bridges often took her on tours of Abilene. She was amazed how few people were on the streets, because in China, streets are crowded with people. Charlotte and I were on a tour with Olive one afternoon, and afterwards she came over to visit me in my apartment.

One day I took her on a half-day visit to the West Texas Rehabilitation Center. We rode the Rehab Center's van there and back. I thought this would give her an idea about one means for patients to get from their homes to the center. She seemed to enjoy the ride. John Thomas and I took her on an extensive tour of the Rehab Center. That was quite a treat for her. John Thomas explained about all aspects of the Rehab Center. She seemed impressed, and kept asking where the people were. Many were at a workshop that day, and I'm sorry she didn't get to see the Rehab Center in full operation. Later, she kept asking Dr. Bridges and me questions about the Rehab Center, so we could see she was really quite impressed and interested. After she returned home to China, we began exchanging letters.

Sometime during 1993, I lost my coordination; this was a source of much frustration. Eventually, I could no longer walk. Now I am able to use a walker or a wheelchair. One morning while preparing breakfast, I dropped a jar of applesauce all over the kitchen floor. It was a real mess, and it took a while to clean it up.

I had to call to cancel the van pick-up, and then call my boss to explain what had happened. Soon, I was dropping pills as well, and then one day fell into a glass picture frame. Bleeding badly, I called 9-1-1 and Debra Guerra came to assist me. Personnel from ambulances, fire trucks and police cars showed up to check on me. Friends joked that this was one way to get the attention of ten good-looking men. I assured them this was not a matter of choice! I stayed with some friends and my adopted mom and dad during those trying days. They had to sew my leg up and brought me back home.

I knew something was the matter with me, so I made an appointment at Scott and White Hospital. Linda, Jared's mother, drove me down there. Dr. Nesbit, head of the Drug and Alcohol Rehabilitation, and I were both stubborn. I realized I needed to be off some of my medication, but I couldn't go off of all of it. While I commend him for his efforts, I also know I have been on medication for more than 40 years.

I kept telling him that a sleeping medication called Halcion was causing my problems, but he refused to listen to me. (Cerebral palsied people are tense, and this is a horrible way to go through life. Most people don't know this.) Anyway, Dr. Nesbit succeeded in taking me off all medication, and soon I felt like the devil.

Another patient, Phil, said, "Jan, you don't look like you feel well at all." I told him he was exactly right. All the while, nurses were trying to get me to do more for myself than I could possibly do. I thought to myself they didn't realize that without medication, I am completely helpless. I tried to tell them, but they simply wouldn't listen.

I had to go to AA, too. Two African American girls there were of considerable help to me. They were both characters. One of them, when asked what she'd like to do when dismissed from there, said, "I'd like to help Jan." I'm glad I made an impression on some people while I was there.

One of the nurses, Katy, was a real character; we had lots of fun together. I'd say she was an "acorn nut." Upon entering my room one day intent on teasing me, she didn't know I had a tape recorder. She was messing with it and buzzing the nurse's station. A few minutes later, a troop of nurses rushed into my room, acting as though they were tying Kathy up to drag her out of my room. As they were dragging her out, Kathy begged, "Jan, help me!" I answered, "Sorry, I can't help you." I wondered if my room was the only one this had ever happened in. I had an idea it was.

After two or three weeks of arguing with the doctor, I came home and got the same precious nursing agency to come back and stay with me. Most of them are good, and some, of course, are bad. I had an infection at home, and they couldn't seem to get it cleared up.

As much as I hated to, I called Dr. Nesbit to inform him about the problem, and he wanted me to return to Temple and come back down there. So I asked the head of the nursing agency if there was anyone, who could take me. Katy, the head of nursing, said they didn't have any cars, but that someone could drive if I'd rent one. I did, and you wouldn't believe who they sent to drive it. She must have weighed 400 pounds, and said she had fallen and hit her head that morning, thus explaining her dizziness. And this would be the person assigned to drive me to a medical appointment 200 miles away! Oh, brother! She cursed all the way down there. Cerebral palsy people have trouble with their nerves anyway, and I was a nervous wreck by the time we arrived.

The intern who saw me could tell that I was fit to be tied, and he asked what was wrong with me. I told him! He failed to understand the problem and I seemed to run into him at every stop in the hospital. Well, a few days after treatment there, the problem cleared up. The doctor and I continued to argue every day.

I had my fiftieth birthday while I was there. I did not want to be in the hospital on my birthday, especially because of several of the people, not that there was anything the matter with the doctors. Most of them, however, simply didn't understand cerebral palsied persons, at least not the ones in that part of the hospital.

It turned out to be a pretty good birthday, though, because Dr. and Mrs. Bridges drove all the way to Temple and brought me a birthday cake as well as presents. People from my church sent birthday cards, and one of the nurses gave me a clown doll. Dr. and Mrs. Bridges also took me out for a most enjoyable meal.

About two or three weeks later, I came home. Wanda, John, and Charlotte came after me. I came home to the same nursing agency that had helped previously. What an experience! I hope I never have to do that again. They stole my diamond necklace and my granddad's pocket watch. They couldn't have stolen anything for which I had more sentimental attachment. It is awful when someone comes in, paid to help someone sick, who steals their stuff. They do so all the time, it seems, and get by with it.

I found a doctor who put me back on some of my pills. I felt better and my coordination was better. Soon I could wait on myself again. I still needed help, so I hired two ladies to work for me four hours daily, 9 a.m.-1 p.m. Mary talked me into calling the police. The police came and said, "They were sorry about it," and they said, "That they would see what they could do about it." It made the head nurse mad. Kate said, "I wish you hadn't of done that, because we hold our own investigation." I thought to myself, "You just didn't want anyone to know about it."

I never did get my diamond necklace or my granddad's pocket watch back. One of the nurses put bleach in my humidifier. It made me sicker than a dog, and speaking of a dog, it made my dog sick, too. Discord prevailed with too many details to relate. Despite many problems with minorities assigned to help me, I continued working with the Human Relations Committee, still working on uplifting minorities of all kinds. And our Martin Luther King Jr. Luncheon seems to be getting better every year.

After I fired three women, Dr. and Mrs. Bridges found me a lovely lady named Omega to work four hours daily. They work with the local Latin

American Mission that is affiliated with the First Baptist Church. Omega and her family are members of that church. She is from Haskell; maybe that's the reason we get along so well! We made several trips to Haskell that made us both happy. We got tickled one day when went to see a chiropractor about a neck pain. A friend recommended him. He didn't seem to understand me at all, so Omega came in, and he couldn't understand her, either. So, he put in his hearing aids and talked to both of us. Finally, he laid me out on the table, putting some strange shoes on me. What that had to do with my neck I will never know! I was laughing all the time he was doing that. I hope he didn't notice. When he got through, he stood me in front of a mirror, as if he was trying to line up my body. The chiropractor then said he would have to see my x-rays before he could do anything else.

When he came out to Omega, he got right up into her face. Later, my friend extending the recommendation said the doctor couldn't hear or see, either. Omega said she never appreciated anyone getting right up in her face, and I didn't care for him, either. I had no plans to return, and didn't. I had been to chiropractors all my life, but this one took the cake!

Then I found a girl named Anita to work with me at night and on weekends, but she had problems getting people to keep her kids. She had to quit, so I hired her sister, Mary. Several months later Omega had to quit, because of health reasons. I knew she also had hoped to go to college, so it made me very sad to realize she wouldn't be able to. I loved Omega very much. We put an ad on the church bulletin board and it wasn't long before Marianne Angel took a job with me. I had asked for a mature Christian lady, who wouldn't mind taking my dog out for a walk in cold weather, and she's perfect – a virtual "Eskimo" in cold weather.

She took me to Haskell during spring break. We took her daughters, Marilyn and Linda, along with us, visiting several friends, including Bobby, who was home for spring break. We visited Ruby and Abe Turner, who earlier had converted their home to a bed and breakfast. It is lovely, all decorated in red, white and blue.

We visited Lane-Felker, an exclusive ladies' dress shop. Its owners and personnel have always been so supportive, and at the foundation of folks who have made me what I am today. They are all lovely people, and I particularly remember Hortense, who got me started in the pre-school department at Sunday school. We also ate pizza, did some shopping and visited Aunt Mary in the nursing home.

Marianne and I spent another day in Haskell when we went along. We shopped, then visited Ben, Charlie and Mary Chapman. They are wonderful friends. I love them as much as I ever did. I lived next door to them growing up, and keenly remember playing with their daughter Kay Henry when we were children. Kay is living back in Haskell now, so we, also, went by to see her. We talked about the "good old days," ate pizza and stopped, yet again, at Lane-Felker. Then we dropped by to see Gwen and Duward Campbell.

I, also, lived by them onetime, and that was quite an experience. Duward, clearly a "walnut," is an absolute character who loves to tease me, embarrassing me at every opportunity. Invariably, he asks me about my "love life" at Peyton Place. I tell him I live there all right, but haven't experienced any of the "love life."

One day, after a hard day's work on the farm, he came home absolutely filthy. He insisted on sitting as close to me as possible, knowing I would eventually say something like, "You stink!" I finally did so, of course, and everyone cracked up. They have four wonderful daughters – Kay, Kim, Kathy and Kristin. They are all grown up now, with families of their own.

I told you that Mary is a character, and this proves it. She recently took a trip with her sister Anita and a friend Sylvia. They helped Anita move to San Marcos. They were stranded, though, most of their "fun-filled" days on the road, stranded when their moving truck broke down. The trucking firm owner couldn't send another one to the next day, and they were stuck in the middle of nowhere. Finally, with 1,200 miles behind them and driving all night, they finally arrived. Mary looked pathetic, her hair down to a point in front of her face, make-up smeared all over her face and her dress a crumpled mess. Looking in the mirror, she realized why the service station attendant gave her such a strange look when they stopped for gas in Cisco! She is a "walnut" for sure!

Something weird has been going on in my apartment for some time, and it can't be explained. Back when I was working at the Rehab Center, I found some sun glasses in the wastebasket I keep near the front door, near Taffy's leashes. The first thing I do each day is take a leash down, and the sun glasses were NOT in the wastebasket the night before. Secondly, no one comes to my house wearing sun glasses except Charlotte, and she says they are not hers. The landlady, maintenance man and the exterminator are the only other people who have keys, and they do NOT wear women's sun glasses! Besides, they don't come unless they are called, and I haven't called them.

Then sometime later, I found a paintbrush on my table; it was a small one, the kind used for painting a canvass or ceramics. I used to paint, but haven't for years. Later, I found a TV tube on my dining room table; I had NOT been working on my TV! Another time, I found a child's toy, some change and Cheetos in my air conditioner closet. And I know the maintenance men did not leave them there, because they had not even been in my apartment.

Then the weirdest thing of all happened. A nice pair of women's glasses appeared on my dining room table. They aren't mine, and no one has claimed them. Is that weird or what? My landlady knows I am telling the truth. She offered to change the locks, and I was glad for her to do so. All is well now. I told them at work that I'd heard of people breaking in so they could steal stuff, but not breaking in where they could leave or share it with you:

Chapter 14

* * *

MY TRIP TO HOLLYWOOD, LOS ANGELES, DR. PERLMAN AND DISNEYLAND

The day I lost my coordination. I had a really hard time accepting it. I kept asking God why this had to happen to me. I so wanted to continue working. I started shaking my head in wonderment at the many people who were capable of working who simply didn't want to. I did!

When I saw normal people content to wasting their lives away, I wanted to shake them saying, "Like is too short to waste." I have been a lucky girl to accomplish many goals. I know that, but the more I have accomplished, the harder it is just to sit around and do nothing. Ever since I returning home from Scott and White Hospital, I have contacted doctors all over Texas and beyond who have experience dealing with cerebral palsy adults. Alas, it seems almost all of them are working with CP children with cerebral palsy, not cerebral palsy adults. I think that's strange.

Finally, I found some at Mayo Clinic. I called my movie star cousin, Mary Kay Place and told her about my problem, seeking her help. I knew if anyone could, she could. It wasn't long before she found one at UCLA. Her name is Dr. Susan Perlman. Mary Kay and I were both thrilled that she was a woman doctor, because women doctors are usually more sympathetic than men doctors concerning women's problems.

The doctor caring for me currently, is a very good doctor. His name is Dr. Joseph Dixon. If you ask him something and he has no answer, he is honest to say he doesn't know.

I made an appointment for July 11, 1995, and he was kind enough to send my medical records to Dr. Perlman. Dr. Perlman was very complimentary of him saying he provided excellent medical records.

Meanwhile, I could not get in touch with Paul Williams. Paul and his wife Barbara have been so good to me. I finally found out that he was sick in the Midland Hospital. It really upset me a great deal. I am just glad I went to see them when I did. A while back before that Debra and her daughter, April agreed to drive me to Pecos, so

Personally-inscribed photo sent to Jan by Mary Kay Place, American actress, singer, director, and screen writer. She is known for portraying Loretta Haggers on the television series: (Mary Hartman, Mary Hartman,) a role that won her the 1977 Prime Time Emmy Award for Outstanding Supporting Actress in a Comedy Series.

I could visit with Paul and Barbara. I was very glad that I went when I did. They finally had to take him to the Methodist Hospital in Houston, where Barbara has a cousin on the staff. He was sick quite a long time. He finally died a week before July the fourth weekend. He had a heart bypass and a pacemaker, but to no avail. They had his funeral on Monday, July 3, at the Presbyterian Church in Pecos. Not sure her car would make the trip, Charlotte rented one so we could attend his funeral. The preacher's message was wonderful, doing great justice to the much good he had done.

We went with Bill to his burial in Barstow. We then followed him to Jim Ed Miller's condominium to pay respects to the family. I got to see Caloma, Paul's brother's wife, whom I had not seen in many years. After visiting with Barbara and friends of the family, we drove home, arriving around 5 p.m. It was a long and tiring trip, but one we had to make.

The next Friday I went on another trip. My life-long friend Paula Roberts accompanied me, with Paul and Barbara --along with Calvary Baptist Church --financing the trip. Paula helped with it, too. (She's now married to Gene Wood. They met at Texas Tech, and both of their parents are from Haskell. They have one teenager named Rusty and two daughters, Missy and Amy, who are now attending Texas Tech.)

Anyway, I flew to Albuquerque, NM on July 8, via Dallas. Paula and Rusty met my plane in Albuquerque. It was so good to see them. I had never met Rusty. When we got to their house, it was so good to see Gene, whom I had not seen for a long time. Another character, he is a "walnut." Amy was at home working a summer job.

I had always wanted to visit Albuquerque, but never figured it would happen. I had been to Ruidoso and all over Colorado, but I'd missed Albuquerque. It is a beautiful place, with mountains looming near the city. It was great to meet Amy when she got home from work. I had met her years earlier, when I played with Miss and Amy at Grandmother Free's home in Haskell when they were little girls. We all ate supper and visited. We watched a rented movie, visited some more and then it was time to pack. We got up early the next morning and Gene took us to the airport for an 11:45 a.m. flight that arrived in Los Angeles at 12:40 p.m.

We headed immediately to luggage claim, our eyes peeled for Mary Kay. Sure enough, we encountered her in a matter of minutes, claimed the luggage and were away to eat at Jack Sprat's Café. Their specialty was low cholesterol food. Then, Mary Kay drove us to the UCLA guest house, where we would be staying during the visit. She then gave us a complete tour of the beautiful city of Los Angeles, including places where she had worked in the past. We saw where the Manson murders occurred, and he big "HOLLYWOOD" letters on the side of the hill. We also saw stars' names engraved on the famous sidewalk in Hollywood.

Always a fan of Dr. Robert Schuller, I was eager to visit the Crystal Cathedral the following Sunday. Their volunteer ministry service picked us up, providing a tour of that beautiful place. We arrived at the Crystal Cathedral about 10:30 A.M. Frances Smith, the volunteer, found a wheelchair for me, and it seemed like a dream that we were actually there! We so enjoyed a beautiful soloist, and got to put money in the collection plate at Crystal Cathedral. We sang hymns, enjoyed the summer choir and were so very impressed by the orchestra.

The only "down side" is that Dr. Schuller was away for the summer, but we did get to hear a wonderful sermon by Dr. Bruce Larson. The window they usually open so people can hear the message in cars wasn't working that day. It was hot, but we endured.

When the service was over, Frances took us to the Visitor's Center, a place where visitors are fed. Following the meal, we collected literature and enjoyed a detailed, guided tour of Crystal Cathedral. Later, we were privileged to meet Dr. Larson, who had come from overseas for the summer of preaching. He was delightful.

The grounds of the Crystal Cathedral are gorgeous, with many beautiful statues on the grounds. Paula and I had never seen anything like any of them, and we took great pictures. Paula took a picture of me standing by the statue of Job. I thought that was ironic, since sometimes I feel like Job must have felt in the Bible—both of us have gone through many trials. One outstanding statue of Jesus included his statement to the people, "If any of you is without sin, throw the first stone."…It was my favorite statue.

The Prayer Tower is something to see. The bottom is lined with 12 beautiful marble pillars in different colors representing the twelve apostles. They surround a crystal statue engraved with a scripture verses. Then, Frances showed us the shops on the grounds, followed by pictures where Dr. Schuller's ministry began at a drive-in movie. She also took us to the burial grounds where Dr. Schuller and his family are to be buried. There were places where people were cremated, and the Roger Millers had the fanciest burial place I had ever seen. It was behind a glass with a beautifully painted piano in the background. Finally, Frances took us back to the guest house. During the return trip, we thanked her, and she said, "Anything for the Lord!" We will see her again when we all get to heaven. What a day of rejoicing that will be!

We spent Monday familiarizing ourselves with the UCLA campus. I was provided a wheelchair, and the manager of the guest house responded to our every need. We ate lunch in the UCLA cafeteria. It was a lovely place with good food.

I had written to Mrs. Flora Thornton, informing her that I was coming to Los Angeles, and that I was eager to see her if that would be possible. She invited me to visit the next afternoon. I was thrilled. We had kept in touch with correspondence after Bates' death, so I knew I wasn't going to Los Angeles without attempting to see her.

We took our chances with LA cabs to visit the Olive Garden before returning to the guest house. The first one took us directly there. On the return, we weren't so fortunate. We had been warned they would "run us around" to run up the meter, and he certainly did. Still, we had a wonderful waiter, had a nice meal and enjoyed an overall great experience.

The next morning was the day I had been waiting for a year -- my appointment with Dr. Susan Perlman. After breakfast, we called the van to come and pick us up and take us to the Neurological Department at UCLA, where I presented my driver's license in exchange for a wheelchair! We were early, but before long, there she was, just as I had pictured her. Finally, I was in the presence of Dr. Susan Perlman!

She asked me numerous questions, then examined me. Even she doesn't know why I lost my coordination. She changed my medication, and advised physical therapy to try upon returning home. She spent about an hour with me. Then we exchanged the wheelchair for my driver's license, got some take-out food and returned to the guest house.

It wasn't long before Kay and Mrs. Thornton's chauffeur came to pick us up. It wasn't far from UCLA to Mrs. Thornton's house. When we got there, Mrs. Thornton hugged me and shook hands with Paula. We met

Mrs. Thornton's private physical therapist. She offered us tea and cookies, and we visited for a long while. She asked me what I had found out from the doctor. I told her, and she said she was pleased I had seen Dr. Perlman. I couldn't believe I was in Bates' home. I just wished he had been there to greet me. I had never met Mrs. Thornton, so I was glad finally to have that opportunity. She and her physical therapist showed us the back yard of her beautiful home before giving us a tour inside the beautiful home.

Next came her granddaughter's wedding picture, as well as a photo of her newest great-grandson. His name is Charles Bates Thornton III. We said good-byes, and her chauffeur took us back to the guest house. Mary Kay called later to see what I had found out from the doctor. I told her, and she, too, was glad we went. After so long a time, we went to bed.

I had a college friend who lived in the Los Angeles area, and I was hoping I could see him while I was there. His name is Father John Neiman You remember him—the ginkgo "nut." However, one of the priests was out ill, so he wasn't able to see me. I was particularly disappointed, since he had promised to provide a tour of China Town.

Mary Kay wanted to pay for a bus tour of Disneyland, but it was a 12-hour commitment, and I was afraid I wasn't up to it. Neither did I think Paula and I were up to dealing with Los Angeles freeways. The next day, however, we screwed up our courage, rented a car and off we went to Disneyland!

We said a prayer and made it fine, arriving at the park shortly before noon. For me, it was the answer to a lifelong dream. (Paula had been to Disneyland on another occasion.) After we had lunch, she pushed my wheelchair down Main Street. What a magical place! (We avoided the shops, trying to avoid spending too much money.) I got to see Goofy, but was disappointed not to meet Mickey Mouse. Soon, we were off to Fantasyland and its Sleeping Beauty Castle, and after that, we saw "It's a Small World," where we took the boat ride. Next was the beautiful King Arthur Carousel, followed by a ride for children called Dumbo, the Flying Elephant. We then had fun riding Mickey's Toontown Train.

Then we went to see what they call Critter Country for a boat ride among all kinds of critters then Frontier Land and its boat ride through some pretty scary country. There was the New Orleans area, which I could tell was Paula's favorite part, and another ride was the Mark Twain Steamboat, where we got something to eat and drink.

We rode the Disneyland monorail over to Tomorrow Land and then all over the Disneyland Park. I had trouble getting up to the monorail, but finally made it. They had something of a moving belt that took riders up to it, and when I saw it, I knew it would be trouble. I got over-balanced and nearly fell down. They had to stop it for me. Later, things were pretty much back to normal for submarine and starship rides.

The last stop we made was in Adventure Land; it was most interesting. After a fantastic show featuring bird singing and talking, we had supper before returning to the guest house. We got lost a few times, but a policeman helped keep us on track. It was the end of a long, but wonderful day.

The next day, we were off to the airport and our return flight home. I love to fly! We had to wait on Amy to get off work, but she finally picked us up and took us to their house in Albuquerque. We ordered some food, and it tasted great after a long day of travel.

Saturday morning Paula slept late. Finally, she got up and prepared breakfast. Then she had to go to the grocery store. I stayed at home and watched TV. Amy and Rusty slept late, but they finally got up. Then Rusty helped Paula bring in the groceries. Gene was in the hospital. After lunch, Paula, Amy, and I drove to downtown Albuquerque, so they could sign some house papers. Paula was buying a house in Lubbock, Texas for the girls.

After we got that done, we drove up into the mountains and had a snack. The mountains are really gorgeous. We had just finished eating when we thought we saw a skunk. Paula said, "Isn't that just our luck!" We were just about to leave, when we realized that it wasn't a skunk at all. It was a charcoal-colored squirrel with a white tail. I wished for a camera! We went back home and visited some more. Then we went out to eat at Furr's.

We had to get up early Sunday morning in order for me to catch my plane home. We got dressed and ate breakfast. I had such a good time that I did not want to go home. We arrived at the airport in time for my plane to leave. Paula kissed me goodbye, and I got settled on the plane. I was worried about missing my plane in Dallas, but I got on the plane to Abilene just fine. However, there was something wrong with that plane, so we had get off and board another plane, thus an hour delay.

Wanda and John had to wait on me, but they didn't mind. I was glad to see them. I had not had anything to eat since breakfast, so we stopped at Grande's and got something for me to eat. They brought me home, and I lay down to rest. I surely was glad to get home. Then Lilly came over with her sister and helped me fix my supper. She also helped me with my bath. I watched a little TV and went to bed. The next day Marianne came to work, and we went to get Taffy. Taffy was as glad to see me as I was to see him.

Paula and I have been friends since we were five years old, and we still are, always sending each other birthday cards. My birthday is June 23 and hers is the 25th, so they are easy for both of us to remember! Not long ago, she sent me a beautiful birthday card with words that expressed exactly how we feel about each other. I want to share it with you:

Looking back
Our girlhood dreams have ripened,
and we've learned a thing or two
from hopes we've seen fulfilled
assorted troubles we've been through...
We're looking forward astonished
at how fast the years have flown,
how much we've done, how far we've come,
how-well-mature we've grown.
Our lives have many stories—
countless memories remain
to touch once again with joy
and tenderness and pain.

And still, we look ahead with hope,
for as the years unfold,
there is no limit to the dreams
a woman's heart can hold.
As you celebrate another year,
I celebrate who you are,
the friendship we share,
of memories waiting to be made.

HAPPY BIRTHDAY!
I love you,
Paula Jo

I am still a member of the Indoor Sports Club, a national club for physically disabled people. We had the club's National Convention in Abilene on August 6-13. I had never been to a National Convention before, and it was a grand experience, getting to meet some interesting and motivated handicapped people. They have what is called the International Good Sports Club, an organization of healthy people who come alongside to help physically challenged people. We tried to get such a club organized in Abilene, but without success.

The Abilene convention was a great success, thanks to the efforts of several folks. Of particular note was the work of Gladys Hume, Juanita Flaniken, Michael Flaniken and Rachel Wacker. They had something planned for attendees every day, including a business meeting, along with special activities at night. There was a reception honoring National Officers and entertainment by the Sweet Adelines, a popular local singing group. They also had door prizes nightly. Tuesday night was Casino Night; Wednesday, evening fellowship, and Thursday, Roland Smith and his Road Runners, a country and western band. Roland Smith really gets into his music, and I love to watch him.

I had met two ladies from California earlier--Carol Mutchnik and Peggy Strohmeier. Carol is the National President. I told them both about my visit to California for an appointment with Dr. Susan Perlman. It turned out she is Carol's doctor, too. It is really a small world after all. I told Carol to tell Dr. Perlman "hello" for me, when she got home.

There are also were some wonderful folks from Amarillo--Sherman and Oleta Jones. They raised three adopted children who are all grown now. One, LeeDon, is physically disabled and helpless. They have taken care of him all his life. Isn't that great? On Saturday night, we had a banquet. It was really neat, featuring a great meal, door prizes and a quilt auction.

Chapter 15

◆ ◆ ◆

A NEW WONDERFUL PLACE TO LIVE
AND NEW JOBS

The place where I live now is a wonderful place to live. The people and the staff are so good to me. They love to tease me, too. There are some more *nuts* out here, too. T.J. is a *pecan nut*. He delights in picking on me. I told him one time, "you are so good to me." T.J. said, "It is not intentional." If he isn't a mess! You would just have to know him to understand.

T.J. started a rumor that I go out and get drunk and come in at 2 o'clock or 3 o'clock in the morning waking everyone up. Then everyone picked up on it. The boy that comes and gets me for church every Sunday morning heard about it, and he started teasing me about it. Lance Cotton is a mess, and I have not figured out what kind of a *nut* he is. I think you would have to call him a *peanut*. You should hear our conversation on the way to church and back. We could go to Hollywood and be a comedian act and make millions of dollars, because our conversations are so funny. Every time Lance scores a point with me, he claps his hands just like a little boy.

And the pastor, Brother Wallace, teases me about chopping cotton. I told him one day that I was going to chop Lance's head off and serve it on a platter. He thought that was very funny! Everyone teases me about this getting drunk. I think it is very funny that they would tease a person in my shape about going out partying and getting drunk. The other day I asked for an empty milk jug and Dwayne said, "Are you going to put moonshine in it?" I told him to Shut Up! I drink water out of an empty water jug. It makes it easier on me. If I had a dollar for every time I said these words, "Shut up," I would be rich today. If I haven't done another thing in my life, I have given many people a lot of pleasure, because everyone loves to tease me. Of course, I pick back.

I really needed another job, because I was so bored. I had looked and looked for another job, but couldn't seem to find one. We had, also, prayed about what God wanted me to do next. I had been to our local job placement office here in Abilene, and they couldn't seem to find me a job either. I went back and took some tests and went through the West Texas Rehab Commission Workshop. I hadn't had much luck with them in the past.

I was having a problem with my ears, which caused every sound that I heard to be way too loud. It was about to run me *nuts*. This problem with my ears really got on my nerves. I had been to the ear doctor and Dr. Scott Wofford about it. Dr. Scott Wofford tried his best to find a cure for my ears, because he knew that it was about to run me *nuts*. The ear doctor said, that it was called sensitive ears, there was no cure for it, and I would just have to live with it. When doctors tell me that, I want to ask them, if they could live with it. We had prayed many a prayer about it. I had this problem when I went to the West Texas Rehab Commission Workshop, which made it harder for me to concentrate on what they wanted me to do, and, also, I missed some sessions because of this problem. I told them that I was trying to find a cure for it.

Well, they once again told me that there was no way I could learn to use a computer, and even if I could learn to use a computer, there was no way I would be able to use a computer on a job. A close friend of mine named Ruth knew that it was about to drive me nuts. She was reading the paper and saw an ad about a local place here in town where they did ear candling. Ruth was a saint in many ways. There is no telling how much good she did in her life. She said, "Let's go and try it. It wouldn't hurt to try it." Well, I went and had it done, and do you know my ears cleared up, and my hearing was back to normal. I was thrilled to death. I was now myself again. It was definitely an answer to many prayers.

I still needed a job. My former pastor, Brother Wayne Oglesby, got me a scholarship to go back to Hardin-Simmons University to take a computer course. I got an excellent teacher named Mr. Wayne Smith. Mr. Wayne Smith is a pecan nut. He had a sense of humor, which always helps. We liked each other from the very start. I had a wonderful young, Christian tutor named Chris St. Clair. We loved each other from the very start. I made an A in the course. I was thrilled to death.

Then I went to Cisco Junior College to take another computer course. I got a very good teacher, who had lots of patience. We both liked each other right off the bat. My teacher's name was Mr. Mike Hitt. I also got another good tutor named Donna. She just loved me. I made a B in the course. My cousins, Mike and Vicki Eastland, who live in Arlington, have made it possible for me to have a computer in my home. I have truly enjoyed it.

A man called one day out of the clear blue sky from a local agency here in Abilene. That man was an answer to many prayers, because he actually got out there in the field and looked for a job for me. Most people at these employment agencies don't care, if they find you a job or not. That man really cared about me finding a job.

He wanted me to come in and see him. I did, and the man at the employment agency asked me, "What kinds of jobs I had in the past, and what kinds of jobs I wanted now." I told him everything about me, and what kind of job I wanted. I sure made an impression on him. He told me to keep in touch with him. I assured him that I would. I called him from time to time.

One day in September, the man from the employment agency said that he thought he had a job for me. Then one day he called me and told me to meet him at a certain place, at a certain time. He gave me the address of the place. Well, I met him there. He introduced me to the staff, and said, "Jan wants and needs a job real bad." I told them everything that I done in my life, and that people said I couldn't do. They were shocked at all my achievements. They couldn't believe that I accomplished what I had accomplished. The staff of Just People, Inc. said they would be thrilled to have me be a part of their staff. I told them that I was going on a small vacation, and, if it was alright with them, I would start when I got back from my vacation. The staff of the organization said, that would be fine with them.

On my vacation, I went again to see B.G., a *chestnut*, and her husband Pete. We visited and ate out. I didn't have long to stay, because B.G and Pete were going to a motorcycle convention. B.G. asked me, "If I wanted to go shopping, and I told her that I just wanted to visit with them." B. G.'s cousin, Judy, came over to see me. She went to school with me in Haskell, too. She has a dog with cerebral palsy. That just slayed me. She wanted my advice on what to do medically for the dog. I told her what I thought she ought to do for the dog. That seemed to satisfy her. That was a very lucky little dog. She found her at the pound. She was the only one who would have wanted that dog. Then I went again to see Mike and Vicki, and we didn't do much this time. We just visited and we went out to eat.

Then I went to see some old friends, Bob and Sam, who had just moved from Abilene to Plano to be near their daughter, Nicki and her husband. Nicki is my adopted niece. I got to go eat out with a high school friend named Beverly. Beverly and I had not seen each other in quite some time. We enjoyed visiting with each other. We ate at a cute little shopping mall. Then after we had finished eating, we looked around a little bit in the shopping mall. Then she took me back to Bob and Sam's house. One night, we all went out to eat at a local eating-place. I enjoyed being with Craig and Nicki. We had fun talking and eating together. The food was sure good. The next day, I came home.

About the middle of September, five years ago, I started my new job with an agency called Just People, Inc. They help troubled kids get their GED, and, also, help them get jobs. I knew right off the bat that I had finally found a place that God could really use me in a fantastic way.

We have moved to a new building and received a grant to start a homeless program. I have given my testimony twice and really made an impression on the kids. I give them positive reinforcement instead of negative. They have plenty of negative stuff in their lives. The kids love me and I love the kids. My staff loves me and I love the staff. We have a fantastic staff. I, also, have a fantastic boss. My boss' name is Dr. Mark Waters. He is a very nice man There are some more nuts at this job. Tony is a mess and another Brazil nut.

One day I wanted Mindy to go get me a candy bar. Ever since then Tony has called me "Jandybar." I had been fussing about the students not putting my chair and my fan back when they went to vacuuming. So one day when I went to work, I went to my office space, and my chair and fan were both turned upside down. So I went to go get Mindy and Veronica to help me; however, when we got back to my office space, my chair and my fan were turned up right again. Tony had been up to his old tricks. He also tried to scare me with a fake rat, but to my amusement it didn't work, because I never noticed it. Ha! Ha!

He, along with the other staff just love to give me a hard time. The rest of the staff names are as follows: Mindy, Earl, Dave, Rebekah, Samantha, and Dianne. They had to let Dave go. I sure hated to see him go. We have a teenager, who answers the telephone, and her name is Dianna. She is a mess. We added a student to our staff. Her name is Veronica. Veronica used to answer the phone. I am very proud of Veronica, because she is on the staff. After Dianna left, we have had two other teenagers to answer the phone. Their names are Kisha and Jasime. Marcus also works part time. My staff says, that I am fun to pick on. That is what everyone says.

One of my students who was in my class when I taught at the West Texas Rehabilitation Center recently graduated from Hardin-Simmons University, and I am very proud of him. I went to his graduation and the reception following his graduation. We are hoping that other handicapped people will follow in our footsteps to higher education. I stood and clapped for him when he graduated, and gave him a Hardin-Simmons University car license plate. The following article came out about him in the *Abilene Reporter- News:*

HSU GRAD TRUMPHS OVER
PHYSICAL LIMITS
By Ken Elsworth
Reporter-News Staff Writer

Matt Casey's small body is twisted to the right, his hands are drawn tightly to his chest and his head moves jerkily up and down when he struggles to speak.

Having cerebral palsy mattered very little to Casey on Saturday.

That's when his father, Bill, proudly pushed his son's wheel-chair across the stage and Matt Casey took possession of his Hardin-Simmons University diploma, graduating cum laude with a 3.7 grade point average.

His brain is obviously fine. It's the body that presents some inconveniences, though Matt doesn't see it that way.

"I have never thought of myself as being disabled," he said Friday, while thinking about his impending graduation.

"It really doesn't affect me the way it might others. And going to school has allowed me to develop relationships with a lot of people that I wouldn't have otherwise. "

Cerebral palsy is caused by damage to the parts of the brain that control muscle movement. The damage usually occurs before, during, or shortly after birth.

If Casey is not impressed by his achievements, his professors are. "It was enlightening, educational, inspirational to have him in our classes, " said Dr. Julian Bridges, the head of the HSU's soci-ology department "I wish every student were as conscientious. I plan to stand for him when goes across the stage."

Casey took Veronica Snow's class called adapted physical educa-tion last semester. The course trains physical education instruc-tors how to work with the disabled people.

"He is very bright." Snow said. "He asked questions that kept me on my toes and Matt could answer his own questions from his own experiences. I think he gained the respect of the people in the class."

Casey, 28, a Cooper High graduate, enrolled at HSU in 1997 after graduating from Cisco Junior College.

Despite his love of philosophy, Casey majored in psychology with a minor in sociology. "He reasoned that those majors would more readily lead him to a possible career in counseling." he said.

He said that he believes he has the potential to Help the disabled. "But I wouldn't want to limit it to Just that population." Casey said, "I'd like to work for a while, but I also have aspirations to go to grad school."

He laughs and smiles often and is known for his upbeat out-look. "I try to stay positive," Casey said. "It opens doors."

❖   ❖   ❖

Then I applied for a scholarship from an organization called *SPECIAL PEOPLE IN NEED*. I had to get five people to write five letters telling why they thought I deserved a scholarship. The five people wrote some fantastic letters about me. I have some really neat friends and kinfolks.

I won the scholarship, and Hardin-Simmons University accepted the scholarship, so I went and took another course in Web Programming. I was happy that I got the same wonderful teacher and the same wonderful tutor. In fact, I was lucky enough to get another tutor by the name of Andrew. Mr. Smith has a great sense of humor, which always helps any situation.

One day, I got really tickled at him. Mr. Smith said, "Why can't one of you students come to me when you do not have a computer problem, instead of coming only when you do have a computer problem?" I thought that was funny. Dr. Bridges told Mr. Smith some nice things about me. Mr. Smith told me that he did. One day, he came into the computer lab, where Chris and I were working. Mr. Smith said, "Dr. Bridges and I were just talking about problem students." Chris and I both laughed, because we knew that he was talking about me. I sure did love Mr. Wayne Smith, and I always will love him, too. Mr. Wayne Smith is a *pecan nut*. By the way I made an A in the course. I was very proud of myself.

My transportation is a bus system called the CityLink. It is a bus for handicapped people. The van picks you at your home, and it takes you wherever you want to go. It has been a real blessing to me. The people in charge are Merle, Penny, Charity and Carolyn, and they love me, too. They have a very hard job, and they do a very good job.

One day I was the CityLink bus, when over the intercom, the people in dispatch office said something awfully funny. The people in the dispatch office made the comment, "We don't know what we are doing?" The diver and I cracked up. The van driver said, If they don't know what they are doing, we sure don't know what we are doing. I called Merle and told her what they had said. She sure did laugh. The van drivers treat me so wonderfully, and they love me, too.

Some of the bus drivers like to tease me. Benie is a mess, and he likes to tease me. Benie says that I look like Clint Eastwood. It is because I wear a fanny belt purse, and in the wintertime I wear a tan coat over it. In the movies Clint Eastwood wears a gun and a tan coat over it. Claudia, Mary, and Eddie are all characters, and they like to tease me too.

Eddie is always trying to take me back to my old address just to aggravate me. He also pretends to call someone on the radio to come and pick me up. He also wants to let me out on a corner that is not at my home. He doesn't make anything off me, because I hand it right back to him. Eddie also says that when he picks me up, he draws the short straw.

Less picked me up to take me home, and he was going the wrong way. I asked him, "Are you sure you know where you are going?" Less said he was taking me to Fort Worth. I said, "No, you are not." He finally got me home, but he took the long way around his elbow to get back to his thumb. I recently wrote a letter to the editor saying they need to give the bus drivers a raise. I hope it will do some good. They sure do have put with a lot of problems that I don't think they should have too.

I met a man named Glen Burton. He is a fine Christian man and a character. too. He has a fine Christian family. His wife Sherry has her own computer business in her home. They have three wonderful kids in college. Their names are Brittany, Wes, and Judd. I have never met them, but I would love too. Glen comes over and helps me with my paper work. The first time he came over, I told about my Uncle Harry being mentally ill and hearing voices. Ever since then, when Glen comes over, he makes out like he hears voices. He makes me laugh. I told him the other day that I wished I had never told him about Harry. He is definitely a character and a *nut*. I haven't figured out what kind of *nut* he is yet. I think I would classify him as another acorn nut. He has definitely been a blessing to me. He says I have been a blessing to him, too. We talk on the phone a lot, and we pray for each other.

Then I called a friend of mine named Trudi, and told her that I was having all kinds of computer problems. I also told her I couldn't afford to pay anyone, and she told where to call to get help. I called the number she told me to call and a guy by the name of Mike said he would be glad to come and help me out. He has been a real blessing to me. He has been able to get me out of a lot of tight spots. My computer has given me fits. Mike says that computers are demon possessed. I think he is right. I asked him why my computer at work doesn't act like my computer at home. Mike says he hasn't figured that out yet. I do similar work on my computer at work like I do at home. Mike is character and a *filbert nut*. Mike and Gini are both sweet, sweet people. I invite them to eat with me every once in a while. He has been over here helping me with my computer so many times until it isn't even funny. I have met their daughter and one grandson. I haven't met their other kids, but I would love to someday.

The following article came out in the *Abilene Reporter-News,* regarding my new job:

PUTTING EXPERIENCE TO WORK
BY: Bill Ayres
Abilenian Editor

The children are grown and it is time to enjoy what is sometimes called "the golden years." Except the gold is a little tarnished – circumstances have changed and it is necessary to return to the workplace once again; or perhaps, for the first time.

Young adults are often heard to say, when unable to secure a job, "how can I get experience if no one will hire me?" Later in life the situation becomes turned around, and the phrase becomes, "I have all this experience, but no one will hire me."

There is an organization whose primary focus is offering training, employment and community service opportunities for mature workers. Experience Works, formerly known as Green Thumb, has a variety of programs designed to help mature individuals enter the workforce, secure more challenging positions, move into new career areas, or supplement incomes.

"When a participant enters the Experience Works program for training they can be placed with a 501C non-profit agency federal, state, city or government agencies," said Wendy Brown, field operations coordinator for Experience Works. They work approximately 20 hours a week and are paid minimum wage by Experience Works. The participating agency, known as host agency, provides training and supervision of the participant.

Brown said, a careful assessment of the participant and host agency is performed to provide the best possible training opportunity for the participant and a good 'match' to meet the host agency's needs.

For example, Brown said that in 2001, 56 year old Jan "Camille" Eastland of Abilene came to Experience Works for help.

" She had definite ideas of what type of work she wanted and what training she needed to be more independent and self-supporting." Brown said.

Eastland uses a scooter for mobility and has cerebral palsy, the effects of which some might view as a disability.

"Camille is far from disabled, " Brown said. "Using a computer to communicate effectively, Camille is an inspiration to all who are associated with her. She is a person who never loses sight of her goals "

Eastland who utilizes the CityLink transportation began working on her Bachelor's degree several years ago, even though she was told she would never graduate. It took her 17 years, but in the end she achieved her goal and obtained her degree in sociology.

Brown said, more recently, Camille realized the importance of computer training in today's workplace and again proved naysayers wrong by becoming computer literate. Her latest adventure has her embarking into the world of literature. She currently has a book in progress.

Experience Works was able to place Camille with Just People, Inc., an Abilene faith-based organization. The host agency was able and willing to accommodate her physical needs and provide ongoing computer training to enhance her skills.

"Camille's endurance of 17 years of study to acquire her bachelor's degree in itself is an inspiration to the youth we serve at Just People Inc., since many are "at risk," said Mark Waters, executive director of Just People, Inc. "We are most appreciative to Experience Works for providing Miss. Eastland and also for the help in the reception area provided by participant Rose Collette.

Brown said Experience Works has operated in Texas since 1970 and provides service in 132 rural counties. The program is part of the Senior Community Service Employment program.

The service is open to anyone, based on income guideline, with the largest percentage women.

Brown added that Experience Works tries to secure full-time and part-time positions; with part-time jobs being the most requested. The biggest obstacles are lack of training, heavy lifting, and night driving.

The program is currently overloaded with clerical workers and there are not enough host agencies' positions. Businesses and organizations in need of good, dependable workers are encouraged to contact the Abilene office.

For more information about Experience Works and its programs, call 795-4329 or visit the web site at www.experience-works.org.

❖   ❖   ❖

I lost my job with Just People, Inc. around Christmas time, and it really upset me because I loved my job. I am planning to get another job.

A friend of mine named Debra went to Arlington on business. I call Debra a dingbat, because she is a dingbat. My nickname is Trouble. I have even got a T-Shirt with the words on it *"Here Comes Trouble."* Every time I wear it, people laugh. Anyway, Debra was on her way to give a speech. However, before she gave her speech, she went in a public restroom. When she got in the restroom, she found the commode barely hanging on the wall. She had used one earlier in the day, and it worked out fine. However, the minute she sat on the commode, it came crashing to the floor. Debra thought to herself, "Oh well, I will just get up and go to my room, take a bath, change clothes, and go on and give my speech." However, after she looked around the room, she could see blood all over everywhere from cuts on her skin. So she called one lady on her cell phone, but the lady didn't understand what she meant.

When the lady realized what the problem was, then she called a local doctor. The doctor came and stitched her on the spot.

Making conversation during the procedure, the doctor said, "What were you going to do, when this happened to you?" She told him she was on her way to give a speech. The doctor then told her to give her speech to him while he stitched her up. So she did just that.

Once when I got to my house, I realized I had accidentally messed in my pants. I tried to get Debra to help me, but she wouldn't do it. She told me to call someone else to help me. I told her no. I had to clean myself up. So when I got through she told me what had happened to her, I couldn't help but laugh. It sure wasn't funny to her though. She has a fear of commodes. I don't know what kind of phobia you would call that. I guess you call it "pot phobia." It was funny to me, but it wasn't funny to her.

Chapter 16

◆ ◆ ◆

MY REST HOME YEARS AT CORONADO

I've got some new people taking care of me, Margaret and Milton Dunn. Margaret was here feeding a lady at lunchtime (Mrs. Cox) and we talked a lot at lunch and Margaret flat fell in love with me! Margaret and Milton are a cross between an acorn and a walnut, and so are their children. We all know one nut attracts another nut! Milton is about as goofy as they come. He goes all over town talking like Donald Duck. Kids come up and say "Are you the guy who talks liked Donald Duck?" It can get pretty crazy! Margaret usually just runs the other way.

I was an only child and have always been afraid of my future, since my Mother and Daddy died. Mike is my only living relative (cousin); but, I'm not afraid anymore because I know God will take care of me. I've always been afraid of rest homes. God put me in a really good place called "Coronado". It is a clean rest home, which is very important. I even became Resident of the Month in June 2010. They love me here and treat me like a queen.

Chris Knapp is the administrator. Curtis Callaway is the assistant. Chris told me one time he is a nut! He has to be to be the administrator of a nursing home. Chris is real tall and Curtis is real short. I told them they looked like Mutt and Jeff. Chris is a peanut and Curtis is a butternut!

Curtis' wife, Jennifer, is in charge of records. Gretchen is our Director of Nurses, with a lot of responsibilities. Pat is the secretary and she is a real nice lady. We have two nice maintenance men, Joe and Jimmy; they are both Brazilian nuts. Jimmy's wife, Brenda, also works here. She is such a good person. She has a hard job.

We have some good nurse's aides, but there are so many I can't name them all. If I left anyone out, it would make them mad and I don't want that.

Lana is our business manager and a very wonderful person. Joseph is her assistant; he is a mess! Shelly is in charge of admissions. Amy and Amber are our social workers. They do a great job. Virginia has a huge job – she is in charge of the kitchen. Judy King is our dietician; she has an important job too.

We have very hardworking janitors. They really keep this place clean, which is a job!

Last of all, the residents – they come and go. They are all taken very good care of. Kim and Glynda do excellent jobs as treatment nurses.

As for me – I'm still a nut. Some people think I am retarded. It is so funny to me. For instance, one time I went to the store to buy something – I wrote a check and as I was leaving, the clerk asked "Do you know where you live?" At the mall, in one store, I asked for potpourri and the lady thought I said "Please." I asked her again and she thought I said "I can't breathe." Finally someone told her what I was saying!!.

This is the end of my book, but it is not the end of the rest of my life, and who knows how many more "Assorted Nuts" I am going to run into before my life ends!

EDITOR'S POSTSCRIPT

This book chronicles Jan Eastland's life through 2012. She is now 74 years old and is excited to see this book – a longtime dream – come to fruition. She continues to be a loving, inspiring individual.

More About Jan

As Jan Eastland writes in this book, the word "no" oftentimes goes missing from her vocabulary. When she was discouraged from enrolling in high school owing to her cerebral palsy, Eastland did so anyway. She embraced life's challenges and didn't let her condition define her. This new inspirational autobiography will encourage anyone struggling with similar issues. Eastland learned how to live with her limitations and overcome many of the obstacles created by them, and she knows that you can do the same. Her work illustrates that with a positive attitude and strong support system, people with disabilities can also lead full, rich lives.

❖ ❖ ❖

In her book, Assorted Nuts, Eastland not only recounts her own journey but pays tribute to the many West Texas residents she met along the way. Each had something new to teach her about positivity and perseverance. These "assorted nuts" gave her support, advice, comfort, and laughter during her most difficult challenges. Though Eastland has demonstrated amazing dedication during her struggle with cerebral palsy, she acknowledges that she certainly couldn't have done it all on her own. She's eager to introduce you to the wonderful people who helped her along the way.

Jan Eastland was born in Garden City, Kansas, and raised in Haskell, Texas. She graduated from Hardin-Simmons University.

Eastland has cerebral palsy but never let that stop her from achieving her dreams. She is determined to show others the amazing courage and perseverance of people suffering from physical impairments